MW00488098

TROUT AND
THEIR FOOD

TROUT AND THEIR FOOD

A Compact Guide for Fly Fishers

DAVE WHITLOCK

Preface by NICK LYONS

Skyhorse Publishing

Copyright © 2010, 2014 by Dave and Emily Whitlock Fly Fishing
Preface copyright © 2010, 2014 by Nick Lyons

All rights reserved. No part of this book may be reproduced in any manner
without the express written consent of the publisher, except in the case of
brief excerpts in critical reviews or articles. All inquiries should be addressed to
Skyhorse Publishing, 307 West 36th Street, 11th Floor, New York, NY 10018.

Skyhorse Publishing books may be purchased in bulk at special discounts for
sales promotion, corporate gifts, fund-raising, or educational purposes. Special
editions can also be created to specifications. For details, contact the Special
Sales Department, Skyhorse Publishing, 307 West 36th Street, 11th Floor,
New York, NY 10018 or info@skyhorsepublishing.com.

Skyhorse® and Skyhorse Publishing® are registered trademarks of Skyhorse
Publishing, Inc.®, a Delaware corporation.

Visit our website at www.skyhorsepublishing.com

10 9 8 7 6 5 4 3 2

These chapters originally appeared in *Trout*, the official publication of Trout Unlimited.
We are grateful to that great organization for facilitating our use of this material.

Paperback ISBN: 978-1-62914-530-3

Library of Congress Cataloging-in-Publication Data
Whitlock, Dave.
  Trout and Their Food: a compact guide for fly fishers /
Dave Whitlock.
     p. cm.
  Includes index.
  ISBN 978-1-60239-693-7
  1. Trout fishing. 2. Trout--Food. 3. Aquatic insects. 4. Flies,
Artificial. I. Title.
  SH687.W5294 2009
  799.17'57--dc22
                                2009012549

Ebook ISBN: 978-1-62636-778-4
Cover design by Adam Bozarth

Printed in China

CONTENTS

CONTENTS

PREFACE

Another helpful book by Dave Whitlock! What a happy occasion for both beginning and advanced fly fishers. No one I know speaks in a more down-to-earth and genuinely practical way about the foods trout eat . . . and illustrates what he says with more graphic clarity and helpfulness. With Dave, artist, fly fisher, teacher, and writer always combine to give us a unique learning experience.

For those just beginning to fish with flies, this little book can be the portal to a lifetime of more satisfying time on the water, introducing the broad range of foods trout eat—and how we might best imitate them, for Dave is also a master fly tyer. And for fly fishers who have been on the water for some years, this book

will surely expand their knowledge in a number of ways: exploring foods not frequently spoken about, the actions of live naturals, the habits of trout in relation to the foods.

This is a fisherman's book. It is not a thorough treatise on all of the trout foods or even one that focuses primarily on the two most popular aquatic insects: mayflies and caddisflies. There are many books on those foods, several of which Dave has written himself—and the serious trout fly fisher will eventually want to study those carefully. What this book does is something unique. In word and extremely helpful illustration, Dave keys in on the major categories of trout foods: aquatic insects, crustaceans and other annelids, a wide group of terrestrial insects, and vertebrates like minnows.

His presentation is never divorced from the life of the entire ecosystem of the stream, or the weather, or the nature of the water. He looks thoughtfully at the life of trout, from birth to its rise forms; he examines how temperature affects a trout's behavior, and how a fisherman can learn to "read" a trout stream.

In sum, in distilled form, readers will have the benefit of Dave Whitlock's more than six decades of observation, experimentation, teaching, and time on the water. Kudos to Trout Unlimited for first printing this invaluable material. I can't think of better shoulders to stand upon than Dave's.

—Nick Lyons

Introduction

Fly fishing can offer a lifetime of great experiences pursuing trout as well as fishing for all the other species. Whichever fish you pursue, the first key to the best results and rewards catching fish on flies begins with knowing what they eat, how that food form lives, and then choosing or tying an imitation that fits the situation best.

Fish, especially trout, feed on an amazing variety of natural live foods every day. Along with immature and adult aquatic insects, they eat terrestrial insects; other invertebrates like annelids (worms), leeches, crustaceans, snails; and vertebrates such as small fish, rodents, and even young birds. By observing the water in which you plan to fish, you can determine what possible foods are present and in what abundance. If you can simply identify the size, color, and shape of what you'd like to imitate and then pick a fly that looks similar to it, you're on your way. Then as you learn the actions of that food form in or on the water and learn to present and fish that fly accordingly, you'll often find fish eager to take your imitation. And that is much more satisfying and fun than if someone else makes those decisions for you or if you just, by experimental accident, hook up with a trout. This process and understanding takes fly fishing to another wonderful level.

To begin this process with the most pleasure, stay within your comfort zone of curiosity and learning. Don't over-complicate it but let time and success lead you to each level of identification. Each time a trout takes your fly, the rush and excitement will have you eager to add to your skills and knowledge of more fish foods and imitations.

By presenting this basic series of fish foods and imitations, my intention is to provide a sound platform from which you can begin learning this subject without its intimidating complexity. I've focused on each major food group that is important to trout and, for that matter, many other freshwater predator and omnivore fish.

Since flies are not real food, you should remember that once you tie on a chosen fly it's up to you to give it lifelike movements in the water; this is needed to convince a fish with your skills of animation and line control that it is truly edible. This takes us back to the observation of live fish foods. This book can show and tell you about each food form and then, with that basic understanding, actually watching the behavior of these living critters in and on the water will make it so much easier to make your own flies act like the real thing. Some naturals merely float dead-drift; others flutter, wiggle, dart, crawl, or act in some other specific way.

It's such a remarkable game we play with nature and fish every time we go out with our fly rod. No two days are ever alike, even if you're blessed with almost seven decades of fly fishing, like I have been. The key to this fascination and to the deep respect we should have for trout is understanding how they live, how they react to their environment, and what they feed on day to day. I hope this book helps guide you to a lifetime of successful experiences in this joyful spirit of fly fishing for trout.

With pen, paint, and heart,

Dave Whitlock

March 2009

ONE

The Trout's World

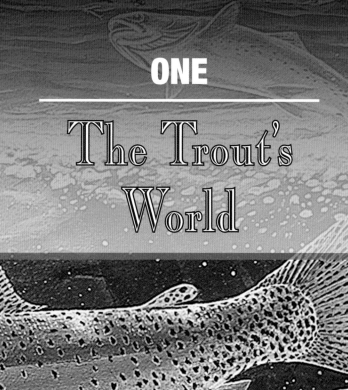

BIRTH OF A WILD TROUT

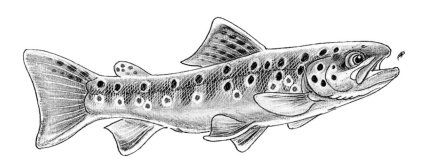

The birth of a wild trout is an incredible climax to a long, complicated chain of events. Knowing these events makes the capture of a wild trout so much more meaningful and reminds me why such a fish is precious.

A wild trout, by my definition, has been naturally reproduced by the physical pairing of trout that have naturally reproduced in the wild for several generations. The life of a wild trout begins when prospective parents become mature and laden with eggs or sperm. This first occurs when the male is two or three years old and the female is three or four. The variation in sexual maturity helps ensure that the parents' genes will not be identical. It is also one of nature's ways of neutralizing weak, recessive genes.

Each family of wild trout has a specific seasonal spawning time. For the most part, in the northern latitudes, brown trout and brook trout are fall and early winter spawners. Trout native to the western slopes of the Rockies, such as rainbow, cutthroat, golden, and Apache, are late-winter to spring spawners.

About two weeks to a month before spawning, adults gather and stage an upstream movement toward the area where they themselves were born. Some trout pair during this staging while others pair later, near or at the nesting site. The movement to the spawning gravels may be as short a distance as a few hundred yards to many hundreds of miles. It's been established that approximately 70 to 80 percent of wild adults find precisely the area where their parents made the redd (nest) and deposited them as eggs. The remainder go elsewhere, not because they're lost, but, I believe, because they're programmed by nature to ensure genetic diversity and species distribution.

When the adult pair reaches the spawning area, which is usually in the shallow gravel area at the tail of a pool, they look for a significant concentration of gravel the size of a marble to that of a walnut. The female makes a trial dig with her tail to test her ability to dig and, even more significantly, to ensure that there is good percolation of water through the gravel. If there isn't, the eggs she deposits there have a very poor chance of incubation. Eggs need a steady flow of constant temperature and oxygen-enriched water to resist fungal attack and freezing. A wild female can choose these perfect areas, while often a hatchery-domesticated female has lost her natural ability to do so!

Next, the female digs a depression in the gravel, with strong tail-thrusts, that is about the size of her body depth and length. As the digging occurs, two other amazing things happen. Directly below her, moved by her tail and the current, a mound of correctly-sized gravel occurs, which is simultaneously washed and cleaned of harmful suffocating silt, sand sediments, and fungus.

Lying in the depression, the female is then joined by her mate. Tensing her body into an arch, she begins a series of 50 to 100 egg ejections into the depression as her mate, pressing close to her, sprays them with milt (sperm). A few small, pale amber eggs are washed downstream, but most settle on the depression or are caught below in the gravel-mound crevices. Other males, immature trout, minnows, and sculpins will immediately move in to eat as many of the eggs they can. The male will try to chase the relentless egg thieves away. Every few minutes the female will dig more gravel just upstream, again causing cleaned and sized gravel to wash back into the rear of the nest, covering up the exposed fertilized eggs. Over a period of just hours to a couple of days she continues the series of digging, depositing, and covering until all 2,000 to 6,000 eggs are laid.

The female and her mate expend an enormous amount of energy and body weight to accomplish mating. Lying fully exposed in shallow water, they are constantly harassed by other males, egg-eating predators, and trout predators like coons, mink, herons, bear, otters, and man. Their bodies, even if they survive, are physically stressed, cut, bitten, and bruised.

BIRTH OF A WILD TROUT

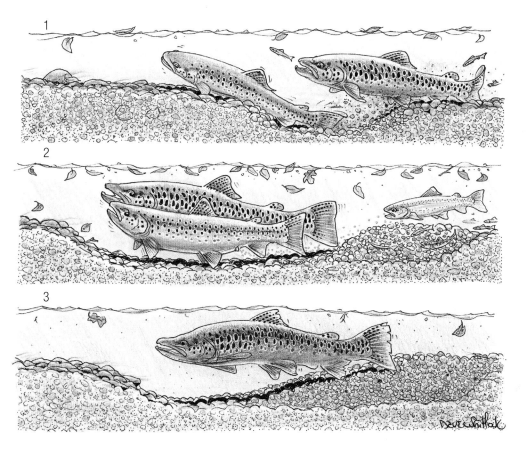

1. The female trout picks an area at the tail of a pool that has good gravel, water percolation, the right-sized stones, and is easy to dig. She builds her nest.
2. Having dug a depression the length and depth of her body, the female is joined by her mate. She lays a series of eggs and the male fertilizes them. Some eggs will be eaten by predators while others are deposited in the crevices in the gravel of the nest.
3. After the egg-laying, the female leaves but the male remains to guard the nest or mate with another female. Eggs will incubate for several months before hatching.

The female will leave the nest soon after the eggs are deposited, but the male may remain longer to protect the eggs or find another mate. Fungus often attacks the tired and stressed parents, bringing a slow death or long postnatal recovery. Of the eggs that are laid, fertilized, and covered up, another 30 to 50 percent are lost to predators. Any eggs that were not covered or eaten soon die of the sun's ultraviolet radiation.

In the next 60 to 90 days (depending on water temperature), the soft, rubbery eggs will incubate. Those that lie in dead-end crevices will suffocate or be devoured by fungus and bacteria. Gravel-mining predators like stonefly nymphs, Dobson fly larva, crayfish, leeches, madtom catfish, and sculpins, continue a non-stop search for surviving embryos. The remaining eggs will hatch into delicate, yolk-sac laden, transparent, larva-like fry.

While in the gravel, the egg sacs of these tiny hatchlings are slowly absorbed by ingestion as they grow into three-quarter- to one-inch-long fry. At the completion of this growth, the fry must escape their gravel tunnels before they use up their yolk reserve and swim to the surface to gulp in air and inflate their swim bladders. If their swim bladders are not inflated before the clock runs out, they are exiled to a short, non-swimming life along the stream bottom. As they attempt their swim to the surface, predators await to make a quick meal of them.

When the fry emerge, if the parents have not deposited the eggs in shallow and slow enough water or if a tailwater is generating high water or the stream is in flood stage, they have little or no chance to safely reach the surface in the strong current. The last emergence obstacles—predators

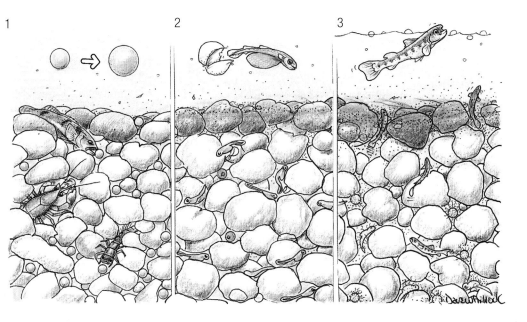

1. Newly laid eggs absorb water and soon double in size and develop a tough, rubbery shell. Gravel predators mine the nest for fresh eggs.
2. Eggs incubate in gravel, develop dark-eyed embryos, and then hatch into larvae-like, egg-sac fry.
3. Fry that have absorbed their yolk sac must make their way up through gravel, penetrate the surface of the stream bed, and swim to the surface to gulp air to inflate their swim bladders. They can then swim and feed as wild trout.

and swimming to surface—take a big toll on the 20 to 30 percent of the fry remaining.

Experts say that even under the most ideal conditions only about 10 to 15 percent of the eggs deposited reach the successful swim-up or free-swimming fry stage! Of those, less than 50 percent survive the first year of their lives. Consider this: every minute of a 24-hour day, the fry are in peril of being eaten or killed. Add to that the burden of finding enough food to survive and grow another day.

A wild trout that grows large enough for us to enjoy fishing for is simply far too superior, precious, and rare a treasure to kill. Wild trout are genetically and environmentally nature's distillation to its finest, most specialized degree of capability to reproduce future wild generations.

So when you are fortunate and skillful enough to catch a wild trout on your fly, treat it thoughtfully with respect and kindness, and carefully release it so it may continue its destiny to grow larger, stronger, and reproduce more generations of wild trout.

STREAM LIFE WITH A TROUT I

Stream trout live in an incredibly different environment than you and me. When I began experiencing their world as they do, my respect and knowledge of them increased greatly, and so did my success in fly fishing for them. To accomplish this, I enter their world and quietly spy on them. To submerge in the chilling 50 to 65 degrees Fahrenheit water where trout live, and to see and breathe there, I equip myself with a neoprene wetsuit, hood, gloves and booties, weight belt, face mask, snorkel, and swim fins.

When I first put on all this gear, I feel as if I'm in some sort of spacesuit. But as soon as I go below the surface and into the stream's swift current, the equipment restrictions seem to disappear. I'm now truly in a different world and suddenly my emotions and heart rate rise rapidly. I feel the pressure of the transparent liquid atmosphere against my face and body, and it quickly becomes comfortable and almost soothing. Sounds that seem greatly amplified surround me and as I stare, wide-eyed, I can see colors and objects clearly for six to ten feet. Objects farther away are in hazy focus and muted colors, eventually forming a blur in the water's turquoise-green tint. Everything seems to be rushing toward and past me. Even shafts of light in the water column and the bottom below me seem to race by. After a minute or so my body begins to warm up, my heart rate slows, and my breathing becomes slower and deeper.

At a distance I see the first trout. It appears to be a shadowy green form gliding just off the bottom. As quietly as I can, I move closer. The fish begins to take on more body and color details. Then at a point determined by the trout's caution of me, I can move no closer. Its 10-inch or so length seems in constant, effortless motion as if it were soaring above and into the water's current using some invisible energy source. Yet for me to remain in a position to observe it, I must kick hard with my fins and hold tightly to the bottom rocks. But then, of course, my body is neither shaped nor lubricated to eliminate the water's force and friction as the trout's is so well-designed to do.

When I'm in the environment of trout, I never cease to be amazed by and learn from them. As the minutes pass, I become less emotional and begin to see the fish and their world more objectively. I begin to see more like a trout. I can best describe the experience as being in a watery wind storm with the unrelenting force of the current and with all sorts of tumbling objects that suddenly appear out of the upstream haze and speed toward and past me. Leaves, twigs, strands of algae, stems of aquatic plants, silvery pearls of air bubbles, insects . . . all drifting and tumbling in one direction and in all levels of the water column.

Looking at the stream surface from below gives me the illusion that I'm watching a time-lapsed sequence of swiftly moving skyscapes. But

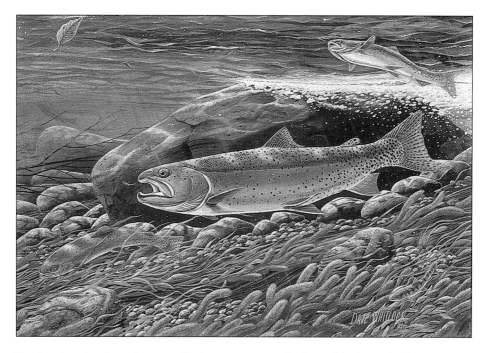

Trout swimming in a clear, sunlit stream can see shallow objects and colors clearly; distant objects fade into the color of the water.

there's something drastically different about the sky roof of the stream. I can only see a relatively small irregular circle of very distorted blue sky, clouds, and shoreline trees. And most of the underneath surface of the stream is an equally distorted reflection of the stream bottom!

If this is what a trout sees when it looks upward at the stream surface, how can it see objects moving above the surface well enough to leap through the surface and eat them? My most educated guess is that trout have extremely keen eye and body coordination and that they are "in the zone" all of the time. I'm so often amazed as I watch trout magically leap through and above a heavily riffled, fast-moving stream surface to snatch flying caddis, mayflies, damselflies, and dragonflies . . . and even my dry

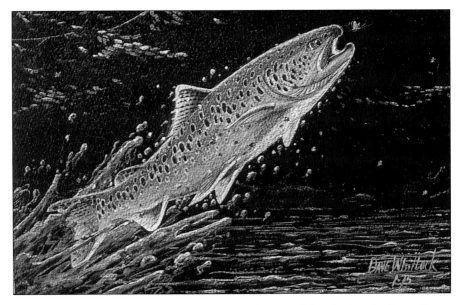

Amazingly, trout can see objects like small insects flying in the air above them through a small distorted window, and they have the ability to leap through that surface and catch them. They also use this same ability to detect airborne and land dangers.

flies! Trout seem to have a sense that biologists have yet to discover. If you've viewed the water's surface from below, you'd probably agree that it seems like trout have extrasensory perception.

When I'm lucky enough to find several trout holding just off the bottom, I am always transfixed by their behavior and their curiosity to the objects drifting toward them. The younger fish are the most active, zooming forward, right, left, down, or up to meet the objects at least halfway. Older trout are much less excitable and much more conservative with their observations as well as the distances they will move to intercept drifting morsels. More on that later.

TROUT'S SIGHT BELOW AND ABOVE THE SURFACE

1. Light rays penetrate surface of stream through a 96-degree arch angle. This is usually known as the trout's surface window.
2. This surface window is distorted by how wavy or rough the surface.
3. The area blind to trout varies 10 degrees from surface (plus or minus 10 degrees) according to how smooth the surface.
4. If the surface is smooth, trout cannot see objects at a lO-degree angle above the surface.
5. Surface area beyond the 96-degree cone of vision is a reflection or mirror of the bottom.
6. Trout can see objects clearly in the water column.

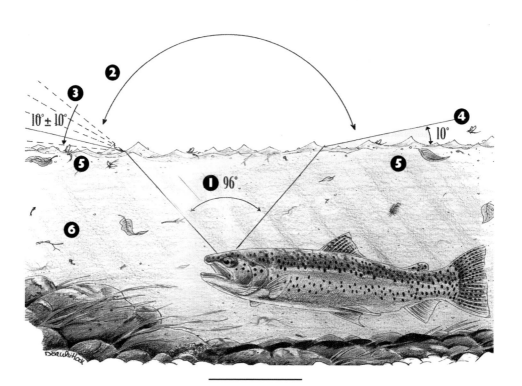

My advice to anglers: always keep in mind that stream trout live in a constantly moving watery atmosphere, and they have highly evolved senses to detect and catch foods. Get into the water with them so that you can visualize their world as they experience it. Through that understanding you'll become a more successful angler.

Stream Life with a Trout II

The surface reflections of a trout stream reveal some of its subsurface secrets, and one of the most intriguing and perplexing is the variation of water speeds from top to bottom.

As water flows down the gradient of a steambed, it moves with variable speeds depending on the degree of the gradient and the friction it encounters as it flows downhill. The steeper the gradient, the faster the water moves by a particular point. At the same time, as the water moves by that point, the speed of the vertical column of that water can vary considerably from the surface down to the stream bottom. It's very important to understand these vertical speed variations to better comprehend the reasons that fish live and feed where they do and how best to present and fish your flies.

Vertical current speeds, or current speeds from the top to the bottom of the water column at one point, may vary from, for example, three miles per hour at the surface to nearly zero next to the bottom. This variation is a simple function of water moving fastest where there is the least friction,

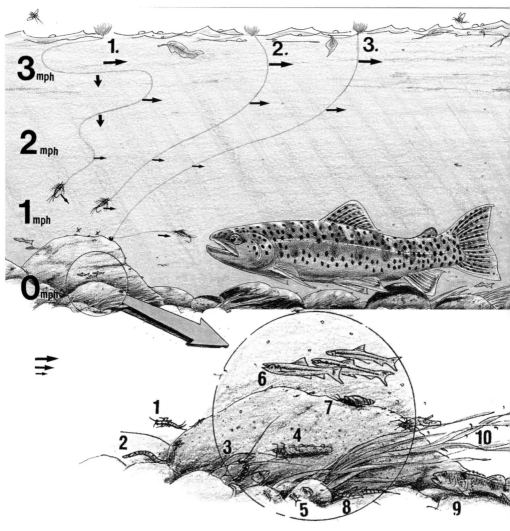

3 mph

2 mph

1 mph

0 mph

1. 2. 3.

6 7 4 1 2 3 5 8 9 10

Can you identify the aquatic trout foods shown in the enlargement?

1. mayfly nymphs
2. leeches and aquatic worms
3. crayfish
4. cased caddis larva
5. scuds and sowbugs

6. minnows
7. snails
8. stonefly nymphs
9. sculpins and darters
10. midge larva and pupa

The top diagram on the facing page shows vertical current speeds and their effects on trout, trout foods, and subsurface flies.

Current speeds are proportional to the stream's gradient and the friction that water is subjected to as it moves downstream and encounters air, water, and stationary objects. Generally, the fastest current will be at the surface, slowing vertically as the water nears the stream bottom.

Trout in a particular area of a stream, especially in riffles, pockets, and runs, will hold just off the bottom where current flow is modestly slow. Most aquatic trout foods live in this area for the same reason.

When presenting a nymph to a feeding trout, anglers should remember that vertical drag especially affects how a subsurface fly sinks and the speed and direction it drifts to the fish:

1. A long, thin tippet presented in a slack coil or pile allows the weighted fly to sink faster than a straight tippet presentation.
2. The fly will have drift speed proportional to the extent of the vertical drag that the tippet encounters between the surface strike indicator and the fly. The arrows show the extent of drag and where most occurs (at surface and mid-depth).
3. A weighted fly and split shot combination will allow the fly to sink into and drift through the feeding zone better and help reduce vertical drag.

which is at the surface where air offers the least resistance. As water encounters water and the resistance of the non-moving objects of the stream bottom, it slows down. The rate of slowdown is proportionate to the roughness or irregularity of the bottom. For instance, sand will offer much less resistance to water flow than will coarse rock, large rubble, or bottom-rooted aquatic plants.

Because trout often look for the most comfort and food with the least amount of effort, they tend to rest on the bottom or suspend close to the bottom where the water current is slowest. Most of their natural foods, such as aquatic insects, crustaceans, and minnows, also choose to live in this zone. The angler who can present and fish his or her flies effectively in this lower portion of the water column will catch trout more consistently.

That sounds pretty simple for successful fishing except that the subsurface stream has its own form of four-letter word, "drag." In this case it's called "vertical drag." If you think the horizontal drag control in dry fly fishing is complicated, add to those surface considerations the current speed variations that the underwater fly, tippet, and leader experience. Wild trout can be just as particular about dragging subsurface flies as they are about surface dragging dry flies! So to be successful with nymphs, emergers, and streamers on your floating lines, it's essential to control both surface and subsurface drag.

Careful mending of the fly line's tip and floating portion of the leader upstream of the tippet or indicator helps to counteract the pull on the line from the surface. The finer and longer the tippet you can use, the faster the fly will sink into the slowest zone while offering the least vertical drag. The water resistance of the fly itself also helps to slow the pull on the fly from above, much like a sea anchor. Extra weighting, such as split shot on the tippet, will slow the downstream drift caused by the more rapid water movement higher in the vertical current column.

Just before I began writing this chapter, I witnessed an eye-opening demonstration of how vertical drag can affect the success of a fly's performance. Two of my students, one a beginner and the other an intermediate-level fly angler, were fishing a very swift 2½-to 3-foot-deep run with a size 6, olive, Nearnuff Sculpin. The intermediate student, who was first through the run, used a 5-foot, No. III sinking-tip line. The beginner fished the run next with a full-sinking, No. IV line. The beginner, using the sinking line, took 10 rainbows while the student with the sink-tip caught only one! I was surprised and amazed at the drastic difference in the success of one form of sinking line over the other using exactly the same fly in such shallow water. Then, after thinking about it, the reason became clear: The full sinker got the fly deeper into the slow layer next to the bottom longer than did the sinking tip, and without much interference from surface drag.

Those wonderful, larger, wild stream trout like to have their food delivered to them, as often as possible, right down where they are most comfortable resting on or suspended just off the scream bottom in the riffles or runs. In that position, within inches of their heads, is a constant, fast-moving conveyor belt of oxygen and food. Placing and drifting a fly on this conveyor belt with as little vertical drag as possible, so as to match the belt's speed, will ensure you consistent success in catching quality trout.

Shade and Shadows

Most wild creatures prefer concealing themselves for comfort and protection in areas with low light. Trout are certainly no exception. Some 30 years ago I witnessed a vivid example of trout hiding themselves in low-light areas. I was swimming in Maine's Little Rangeley River one afternoon in late spring, photographing brook trout in a few feet of clear, sunlit water that was strewn with small boulders.

I took a couple of rolls of 400 ASA film with an underwater camera using only available sunlight. Satisfied that I'd gotten some neat shots of these beautiful, 8- to 12-inch brookies, I was shocked when the slides came back from the processor. Nearly every trout I shot was just barely visible and almost colorless! Why? I looked closer and was amazed to see that each trout was holding in the shade of a nearby boulder. I

To locate trout on sunny days, look for shade and shadows on or below the water. Observe shade curtains created by objects above the water, such as overhanging trees, rock or ledge out-crops, dead falls, floating logs, or root wads. Don't forget shadows created by foam lines, eddy scum, or floating leaves. Below the surface, look for rocks, boulders, ledges, sunken tree trunks, moss beds, and deeper water.

returned to the river a few days later and took a more objective look at the fish. Sure enough, most of the time the fish I located were holding on the boulders' shaded side. They only occasionally moved into the full sunlight to feed or dart away from my approach. None of them held on the boulders' sunny side.

After that experience I began observing more closely and found that most trout I saw in streams, small and large, were associated with some sort of shade cover. I already knew from many years of experience that the best fishing was nearly always when low-light levels existed from either shade lines, time of day, clouds, or deeper dark water. But it was good confirmation to see trout relating to shadows as if they were a form of structure.

Sunlight, of course, provides most of the illumination a trout stream receives, and it is especially intense through the middle part of the day. When sunlight strikes opaque objects like boulders and logs, the object blocks most of it and a shadow results on the side of the object opposite from the sun. Trout do not have eyelids, sunglasses, or even a nice billed cap to shade their eyes from the glare. Also, the brighter the light, the easier predators can see them. If shade is available, that's the most comfortable and safe spot for a trout to hold.

Another example I've seen of trout gravitating to shade occurs each sunny day in a calm pool on a clear spring creek in the southern Ozarks. The bottom of the pool is mostly composed of small stones, gravel, and sand. Between 11:00 AM to 4:00 PM, one particularly tall, nearly limbless tree casts a shadow of its slender trunk across the creek. The rainbow trout stocked there (mostly 12 to 18 inches) line up side by side across the stream in the shadow of this trunk that is just barely wider than they are long! Few, if any, trout lie above or below the shadow.

One of the most bizarre experiences I've witnessed of trout gravitating to the safety of shade occurred one March in a drought-low river on the south island of New Zealand. My wife Emily was on the bank and spotted a very large and very edgy brown trout holding under the scant foam line in the deepest part of a little pool. My first cast spooked it and it swam directly toward the pool's shallow side. We then watched in amazement as this two-foot-long trout swam with at least a quarter of its back and tail out of water to an almost dry, large boulder. The trout simply disappeared in the boulder's dark recess.

Trout will always use shady side of sunlit boulders to rest next to for safety and eye comfort.

As water deepens, it filters out light proportional to time of day, color of water, and its depth. When I'm fishing, I regularly look for the darker areas where the bottom colors and shapes of the sand, gravel, rock, and vegetation blur and become more like the color of the water. Anglers can benefit from the shade and shadows, too. I learned to successfully stalk and catch Michigan steelhead by staying in the shade when they were in the sunlight. It's difficult for eyes adjusted to open sunlight to see into darker shaded areas. Remember how hard it is to see in a dark movie theater when you first enter from the well-lit lobby?

Bear in mind that shadows created by air or surface predators can scare trout into sheer panic. Your shadow from your fly line and leader can frighten trout as surely as tossing a stone at them. Do whatever you can to keep your shadows from passing over or coming close to a trout.

When trout do swim into sunlight, you can often spot them quickly by finding their shadows rather than the fish themselves. Using polarized glasses and a hat with a good bill, focus on the bottom for fish-shaped shadows. When you see one, note the sun's angle and bring your eye to focus up off the bottom in that direction: You can then usually see the almost invisible, suspended form of the trout. Once you can see the fish, making an accurate presentation and catching it becomes much more possible.

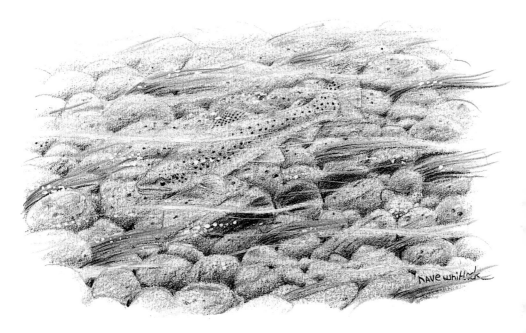

When trout swim into sunlight, locate them by finding their shadow on the stream bottom. Then, note the sun's angle and look up off the bottom in that direction to see the suspended form of the fish.

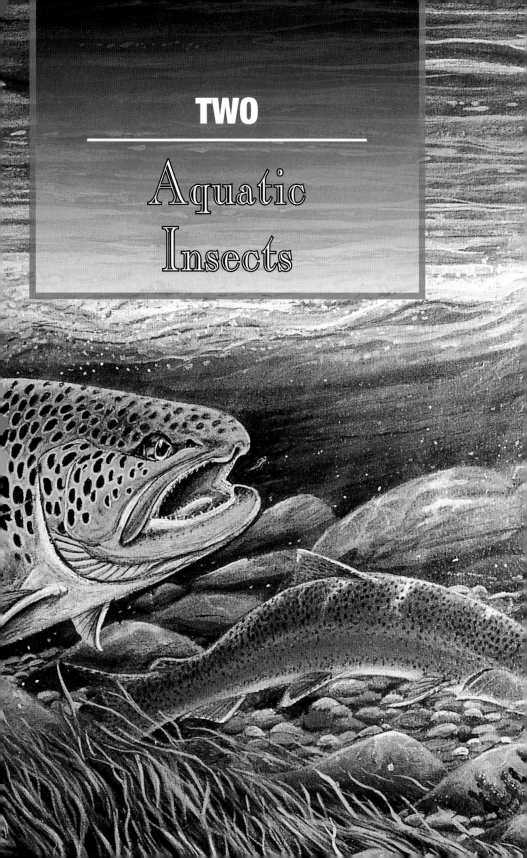

TWO

Aquatic Insects

Aquatic Insects

Historically, aquatic insects have formed the cornerstone of trout fishing. This group of insects populates the majority of trout waters and in most areas provides the most reliable, annual food forms for trout. In fact, fly fishing evolved in Europe over 400 years ago when trout anglers, who used *live* aquatic insects to catch their quarry, began trying hand-made imitations.

Efforts to correctly identify the aquatic insects that are significant to trout, along with their life cycles, and how to imitate and present them to feeding trout have resulted in an amazing, and still growing, number of books and articles about fly fishing and tying. Also, as a direct result, we now have many thousands of fly designs and patterns available.

At first glance, this huge choice of information and flies can be overwhelming to anglers, especially newcomers to the sport, possibly preventing them from enjoying a lifetime of fly fishing and that incredible experience of matching the hatch. I remember when I began to fly fish

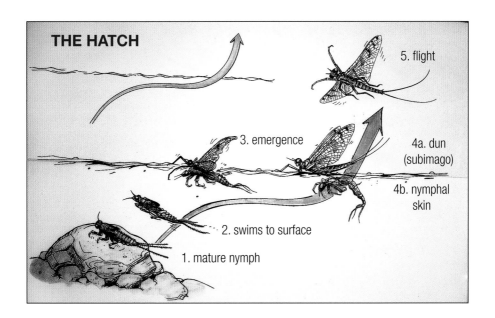

THE HATCH

5. flight

3. emergence

4a. dun (subimago)

4b. nymphal skin

2. swims to surface

1. mature nymph

During hatching, the insect first exposes itself (1) by staging on the stream bottom. It then moves to the stream's surface (2), where it pushes through the surface film (3) and begins to split its skin, soon emerging as a winged, air-breathing adult (4). The new adult expands its wings, which quickly dry out and stiffen for flight. Once this transformation is complete, the adult flies off the water's surface (5) to the stream side until conditions are ready for it to mate. The adult flies back to the water, mates, and lays its eggs on or below the water's surface.

60 years ago, a time when there was far less information available than today on aquatic insects. I was intimidated and turned my back on the subject, avoiding aquatic insects altogether. But eventually I learned a simple working understanding of these most interesting creatures, and it increased my fly-fishing pleasure and successes immeasurably. I'll attempt to make that path clearer for you, too.

What are aquatic insects? They are part of a group of true insects (having six legs) that spend most of their sexually immature life living and breathing underwater, and then most of their adult lives as air-breathing, flying insects. As adults they mate and deposit their eggs on, beneath, or beside their home waters. Generally, once egg-depositing is completed, the adults die.

Since aquatic insects spend most of their life cycle underwater, they are a perfect food form for trout to catch and consume conveniently. In order for these immature, aquatic insects to survive predation, they must camouflage or conceal themselves on or beneath stream structures, such as rocks and aquatic vegetation, or burrow into the stream bottom. Thus hidden, trout must either dislodge them or find times when the insects come out to feed, migrate or hatch, or when they are dislodged from their cover by sudden changes in water volume and speed.

So, what's a hatch? This term describes the period when aquatic insects are the most vulnerable to trout, and when fly fishing, for many anglers, is the most exciting. It is that part of the insect's life cycle when the water-breathing, immature insect transforms into the air-breathing adult. To accomplish this, the insects must depart from their watery hiding places and swim or crawl up to and/or out of the surface of the water, split their outer skins, and emerge as winged, sexually mature, air-breathing adults. These mature insects fly off and mate and then return to the water to deposit their eggs, either on or below the surface. Many aquatic species then die after depositing their eggs and fall back to the surface of the water. Even though this hatch of an individual insect takes only seconds to minutes for most aquatic insects, the ever vigilant and opportunistic

Trout will feed on insects in three stream levels, starting at the bottom (the first step of the hatch), then feeding on insects that are rising from the bottom to the surface, and finally feeding on insects at or above the water's surface.

trout are always watching and will seize and devour them at all stages of this transformation.

Most hatches of a particular species of aquatic insect occur once a year and last for about two weeks on average, with the actual hatch lasting about two to three hours each day. However, some of the smallest species and those species that live in spring creeks or other waters that have a more or less constant annual temperature range, may hatch for much longer periods or even have several generations in one year. Therefore, much of the success of catching trout on flies depends on an angler's knowledge of what is hatching on any particular day or week of the trout season, and determining the size, color, and form of that insect and life-cycle stage.

Trout feeding on daily hatches become selective to the stages of these hatches and often ignore other naturals or imitations that deviate from the stage, size, action, shape, and color of that insect. An angler who is not "matching the hatch" may have a hard time catching very many trout, even though there might be trout actively feeding all around. At times like these, observation, knowledge, and good fly selection are needed.

The better your understanding of aquatic insects during this marvelous phenomenon called a hatch, the more success and satisfaction you'll have fly fishing for trout in the seasons to come. In the next chapters, I'll do my best to improve that understanding for you.

GENERAL AQUATIC INSECT ANATOMY

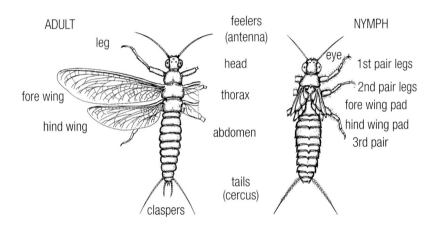

The first step in identifying aquatic insects is learning their basic anatomic parts. Each group of aquatic insects has its own unique combination of these parts.

Identifying Mayflies and Stoneflies

As discussed, aquatic insects are one of the most often imitated food forms used by fly anglers. These are insects that have both an underwater, gilled form and an air-breathing form in their life cycle. It's estimated that the 10 orders of aquatic insects contain approximately 8,000 species. Although trout might eat most of these, there are only 5 orders and far fewer than 500 species that are of significant importance to North American trout fishing. In any given order, many of these species look similar to our eyes, and to a trout's as well, I suspect. That's why they can be imitated with a just a few dozen patterns of trout flies, in several sizes.

While success is possible if you can match the particular size, shape, and color of an insect; it's the correct *action* in the water that might be the most important factor. This requires you to be able to identify the general group into which the insect falls, determine whether the insect is in the immature (underwater) form or the adult (air-breathing) form, and that you understand the action of that stage of the life cycle. Once you know this, you are well-prepared to match the immature aquatic insects as trout feed on them year-round, as well as match the brief hatch when the insects mature and emerge into their adult forms.

Of the six major groups—mayflies, stoneflies, caddisflies, midges, dragonflies, and damselflies—we can break them down into three categories that have similar characteristics in their life cycles. Understanding these similarities will simplify the task of identifying and imitating them. These categories are: mayflies and stoneflies; caddisflies and midges; and dragonflies and damselflies.

Let's begin with the first category, mayflies and stoneflies. There are many physical similarities and some distinctive differences that make these two groups easy to identify and distinguish from other major aquatic insects. First, both have a simple life cycle form of egg, nymph, and adult. Anglers use the term "nymph" to describe the larval form of these two insects. The mayfly is unique in the aquatic insect–world because it has *two* adult forms: the dun (sub imago) and spinner (adult) form. The stonefly, and all other aquatic insects, has only one adult form.

Mayflies: (Ephemeroptera)

Mayflies are the cornerstone of the origin of *fly* fishing. European anglers developed fly-fishing tackle and fly tying through their efforts to catch trout and grayling that were feeding on mayflies. Mayflies are primitive, harmless,

HOW TO IDENTIFY MAYFLIES AND STONEFLIES

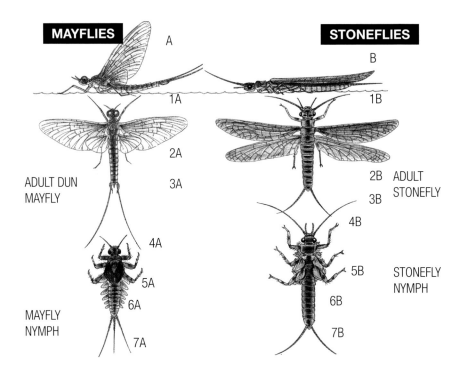

These illustrations depict the general the general shape and color of the adults and nymphs of mayflies and stoneflies. Shapes and color vary considerably with each species.

ADULTS

Insects at rest on water:

A. Adult dun mayfly—Wings are upright and together, resembling a small sailboat.

B. Adult stonefly—Wings fold down and flat over the back of the insect.

Insects in flight:

1A. Mayfly antennae are small and difficult to see while in flight.

1B. Stonefly antenna are large, long, and easy to see.

Wings:

    2A. Mayfly has four wings—two large and two small.

    2B. Stonefly has four almost equal-sized wings; in flight they appear large and clumsy.

Tail Parts:

    3A. Mayfly—two or three long, slender, graceful hair-like tails; usually visible when in flight.

    3B. Stonefly—Two short to medium length, stiff, heavy tail parts, not especially visible in flight.

NYMPHS

Antennae:

    4A. Mayfly nymph has two, small antennae that are hard to see without magnification.

    4B. Stonefly nymph has two large, long, stiff antennae that are easy to see.

Immature Wings:

    5A. Mayfly nymph has two small wing pods over the back that are difficult to distinguish.

    5B. Stonefly nymph has two sets of clearly visible, immature wing cases on the second and third thoracic segments.

Gills:

    6A. Mayfly nymph has distinctive gill structures on the upper sides of the abdomen.

    6B. Stonefly nymph has no gills, but larger species have crude star-shaped gill filaments on the underside of the thorax between the legs.

Tail Parts:

    7A. Mayfly nymph has three distinctive tails on the last segment of the abdomen.

    7B. Stonefly nymph has two coarse, short- to medium-length tails on the last abdominal segment.

fragile, and graceful. The adult's slender, tapered body has two pairs of sail-shaped wings that are held straight up and together at rest, making it look like a miniature sailboat on the water. The two or three long, curving tail parts enhance the mayfly's classic look.

The mayfly nymphal form, though less spectacular, is attractive to fish—they eagerly feed on them all year-round. Depending on the species, these immature forms survive in still or flowing water by swimming, crawling, or clinging to bottom structures or by burrowing into the streambed. Their three tails, lack of easily visible antenna, and gills on the upper sides of their abdomen segments identify mayfly nymphs. If you'd like to check closer with a 4x magnifier, a single pair of immature wings is visible on their anterior thorax. Their colors can be distinctive, but generally they are intricate patterns of tan, brown, olive, gold, and black, which camouflage them in their environment.

Mayfly eggs and young nymphs are of little significance to adult trout because they are so small. But once the nymphs approach maturity, their size increases as does their exposures to trout. This is especially so a week or two before and during their emergence journey to the water surface to hatch. Most species of mayfly nymphs live several months to a year or more underwater and then swim to the surface to emerge into duns. A few transform before or during their rise to the surface. So, either naturally drifting a nymph imitation close to the bottom or raising it slowly to the surface will bring the most consistent strikes.

The nymph, on its way to the surface or at the surface, splits its skin and emerges into the air-breathing, ready-for-flight, adult dun. This first adult stage characteristically rests on the water's surface as its new wings unfold and become rigid for flight. This gives trout ample time to see them and make a slow, deliberate rise to them. The insect then flutters and launches into flight up toward the nearest shoreline to find seclusion to rest. Later, the skin will split again and transform the matte-finished dun into the more colorful, shiny, adult spinner. A few species of the smaller mayflies do this transformation as they fly away from the water right after emerging, but most wait until darkness or the next day to complete their adult form. In either case, the insects form a mating swarm, dancing up and down together, usually over the water. Within minutes to an hour after mating, the females descend and lay their eggs on or below the water. A few species even swim to the bottom and lay their eggs on the sides of or beneath rocks. Both males and females die soon afterward.

Trout make a distinctive, slow to moderate rise to emerging duns and egg-laying females. First the trout's head appears and then anglers usually see its tail come up as the fish arches back down. When the trout take the nearly invisible, low-floating, spent, or dead spinners, you'll see an almost imperceptible rise, with the fish just barely breaking the surface with its nose and mouth. Recognizing these two rise forms is another way to identify which insects trout are feeding on and thus, which dry fly to use.

Stoneflies (Plecoptera)

Stoneflies are predominately found in coarse stone or rubble in moderate to fast-flowing areas of streams. Stoneflies have an inefficient breathing system and must have relatively swift, highly oxygenated water flowing over their gills at all times. They have a simple life cycle of egg, nymph, and adult. However, many stonefly species take longer to mature in their nymph form. The larger species can take several minutes to split their skin and become fully formed adults, so they must crawl out of the water onto stream structures to go through this transformation. The adults then fly or crawl to streamside cover, especially willows and leafy bushes, where they gather and mate. Then the females crawl or fly back to the stream to deposit their eggs in the water along the shoreline or on the water surface, depending on the species. Adults may live a few days to several weeks.

Its roach-like shape (two distinctive and stiff antennae, two stiff tails, and a lack of gills on its segmented abdomen) easily identify the stonefly nymph. Some stonefly nymphs absorb oxygen through their skins and/ or by crude gill filaments between their legs and lower part of their thorax. Most also have two pairs of immature wings on the second and third thoracic segments. Most anglers will quickly identify a nymph as a stonefly if the nymph has two tails and two distinct antennae.

The adults have two pairs of large wings that fold down flat over the top of their bodies when at rest. In flight, these wings appear large and clumsy. The long, stiff antennae and two tails are also a unique physical point of identification of the adult.

Most stonefly nymphs, especially larger species, crawl on bottom structure and seldom swim. Trout, therefore, take the nymph imitation best if it is simply drifted and tumbled near the bottom in the rapid riffle and run sections of a stream. When the adult females return to the water to deposit eggs, most species skitter over the water surface to do so. Trout react to the quick movements of the stonefly by aggressively moving on the fly with mouth-wide-open strikes. When you see this rise form, cast above the trout with an adult stonefly imitation and skitter, twitch, and drift it to the trout.

Mayflies and stoneflies are easy to imitate once you've identified their presence or hatching activities. Successful fishing depends on imitating the correct life-cycle stage along with the natural action of that form. Being able to put that all together and then entice a trout into believing it's real, adds much to the pleasure of fishing.

CADDIS AND MIDGES

C addis and midges live in most trout waters and are often more important as food forms than any of the other aquatic insect orders. But until more or less recently, about the last three or four decades, neither carried much favor with trout fly fishers in North America.

Why? Well, as I see it, caddis simply look like grubs and moths and usually don't rest long enough at the water surface to be classic dry fly opportunities. Then there are the midges which are very small and hard to see and look like mosquitoes. Also until recently, we've lacked the sensitive tackle to fish such micro flies effectively as well as the reliable 6, 7, and 8x tippet that it requires to deceptively present and fish them efficiently. Yet an objective focus on caddis and midges will reveal that they are fascinating aquatic insects that are extremely widespread and often very abundant by numbers and sheer volume in most trout waters. Both can survive more of man's abuses to their waters than mayflies or stoneflies, often even thriving better in murky waters that are created from man's "gifts" of siltation and agricultural nutrients.

So, recognizing their presence and knowing a bit about the parts of their life cycle that are important to trout can significantly improve your trout fly fishing success and pleasure. They, like stoneflies and mayflies, have unique physical characteristics that make each relatively easy to identify.

Caddis Flies (Trichoptera)

The caddis is a more evolved insect than the first two insects we've discussed, mayflies and stoneflies, having a four-part or complete life cycle: egg, larva, pupa, and adult. The adult caddis is a nervous character that looks and acts like a small- to medium-size moth on stimulants. A close look reveals that, when they are not flying, their wings are folded over their backs like a tent or roof. These wings have microscopic hairs on them while look-a-like moths have microscopic scales on their wings. The Latin name for this order, Trichoptera, means *hairy wings*.

The caddis larva has a grub or hairless-caterpillar body look and they live on, under, or below structures. To conceal their vulnerable, tasty forms, many construct protective cases in which to live that are unique to each species. These cases are wonderfully diverse structures constructed from bottom sand, tiny stones, shells, aquatic vegetation, as well as segments of terrestrial grass, leaves, and twigs. Some nomadic caddis build cases that are very portable while others fix themselves permanently to underwater structures.

2A and 2B: Typical portable cases and larvae
2C: Fixed or nonportable case and larva

Some caddis species do not construct a case until they pupate, but instead have camo body color and live more reclusively under the protection of stones, vegetation, or crevices. These free-living larvae are the most often imitated by fly tiers and nymph fly fishers. Trout prefer the free-living species but will also gather and eat many of the easier-to-find, cased larvae.

After the larva matures, it fixes its case to bottom structure or if it has no case it forms a fixed cocoon around itself, seals itself inside, and begins its pupation period of two or three weeks. Once this period is accomplished and water conditions are correct, the pupa opens its case and with its long legs swims promptly to the surface. This ascension speed is helped by expansion of gas underneath the pupa's skin.

The pupa resembles the adult caddis, but without the four long, moth-like wings. Most species of caddis pupa have very long legs and antenna. Just before or as the pupa reaches the surface, it transforms in a blink of the eye, by a shedding its pupal skin before or as it breaks through the surface and becomes the winged adult that runs or flies off the water. The new adult, which is usually light-colored, hides along the edge-water vegetation where it usually becomes darker in wing and body color. Later, after mating, the female flies or runs back to the water and deposits her eggs on its surface, on surfaces of structures in the water, or dives under and deposits her eggs on or beneath bottom structures.

Trout leisurely take larvae off the bottom when the pupae are not hatching, but as pupae begin to quickly ascend, trout become excited and dash up to intercept them, often splashing through the surface in a quick, noisy rise-form that is easy to recognize. They'll also make similar fast, showy rises or even leap above the surface when catching the fluttering emergent adults. It is truly exciting. When the egg-laden adult caddis flies back to the water's surface they dip and skitter or dive into the water to deposit their eggs. If there are many of these ovipositors, trout again become frenzied with catching them. It's a little easier to catch sight of adults at this phase than when adults are doing their Polaris Missile act of emergence from the pupa. Late afternoon, evening, and night time are the best periods to observe caddis ovipositing.

You can see by this description why imitating caddis flies is most effective if you use a type of fly action we often call traditional wet-fly fishing or soft-hackle fishing. Even adult caddis dry flies like elk hair caddis and poly wing caddis are often more effective when twitched, skittered, or pulled beneath the surface. In my opinion, imitating emergent and ovipositing caddis is a very pro-active and fascinating fly-fishing method and one I truly love.

Midges (Diptera)

Midges, like caddis, have four stages in their life cycle: egg, larva, pupa, and adults. These tiny, remarkable insects lack size, but they more than make up for it in sheer abundance in every trout water that I've experienced. And, it is their miniscule size and great abundance that provides what I consider as the most challenging plateau of trout fishing: "midging." Midges, because of the large number of species and annual multi-generations, are available in all stages almost all year-round and so trout can feed on them nearly every day, spring, summer, fall, and winter.

In many trout waters, midges are the main trout food all winter long, causing trout to actively feed on the surface even on the coldest of days. Fact is, in my experience, trout are usually midging even when other larger insects are emerging or when they consistently refuse your size 8 to 18 nymphs and dry flies. If that's the case, try size 18 to 24 midge larva or pupa imitations.

Midge larva are very simple, worm-like forms without visible body parts other than segments. They average about one eighth to one quarter

KEYS TO IDENTIFICATION OF EACH INSECT:

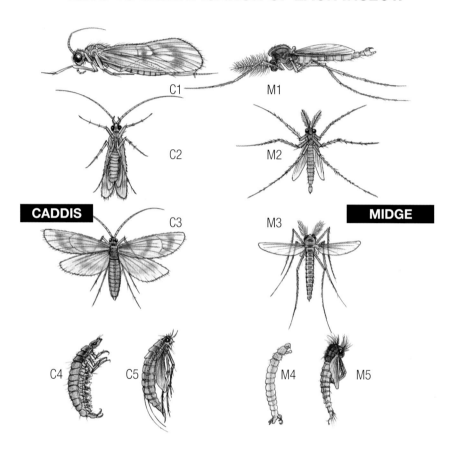

C1

M1

C2

M2

CADDIS

C3

M3

MIDGE

C4   C5

M4   M5

CADDIS (Left)

C 1: Caddis **adult** at rest—**side view.** Wings are folded over back in a tent or roof-like position. Long antennae are very visible.

C 2: Caddis **adult** at rest—**underside.** Two very long antennae, six long legs, and tail-less body. Body is somewhat shorter than wings.

C 3: Caddis **adult in flight.** Two pair of moth-shaped wings, long antennae, and no visible tails.

C 4: Caddis **larva.** Grub-worm appearance with six distinct legs, no visible tails or antennae, and gill filaments are located along the bottom side of abdomen.

C 5: Caddis **pupa.** Looks almost like a wingless adult. Legs and antennae are long, immature wings are visible on lower thorax.

MIDGES (Right)

M 1: Midge **adult** at rest—**side view.** Looks like a mosquito with big, fuzzy antennae and two short wings. No tail parts and a distinctive, large, humpy thorax.

M 2: Midge **adult** at rest—**underside.** Six very long legs, a pair of fuzzy antennae, clearly segmented abdomen, two short wings, and no visible tail parts.

M 3: Midge **adult in flight.** Two small wings that make a distinctive buzzing sound.

M 4: Midge **larva.** Very simple, worm-like body with no visible legs, antennae, wing cases, gills, or tail parts.

M 5: Midge **pupa.** Has large, humpy thorax, with legs and wing cases folded tightly underneath. Head has distinctive gill filaments on it. Abdomen is distinctly segmented and has no tail parts.

inch and live without cases in reclusive colonies on underwater structures, aquatic vegetation, or in stream-bottom muck. When dislodged, most swim very slowly, with a distinctive whip-like action. Trout grub for them or dislodge them with their tails, catching them before they can hide or drift away.

Midge larvae pupate in a simple capsule-like case they construct that conceals them on bottom structure while they transform from larva to pupa. When the pupae emerge, their forms are more complicated than the larva, but less intricate than adults. When they emerge, they slowly rise to the surface with the aid of gas and some simple whip-like swimming movements. Unlike caddis, the pupae emerge slowly and so they tend to gather in significant numbers at the surface film. Slow or still-water species take longer to emerge and obtain flight than fast-water species. Because pupae often linger on the surface for an extended period, trout usually eat more pupa than either larva or adults.

A close look at adult midges shows that they are neat-looking, long-legged, two-winged insects with pronounced fuzzy-looking antenna and distinctive body segmentation. They look much like mosquitoes, but most, thankfully, do not feed on fly fisher's blood like so many of the Diptera order (black flies, mosquito, deer flies, etc.). They make an audible buzzing sound in flight due to their two short wings beating at very high rpm and so British anglers often call them *buzzers*.

Trout eat the adult best if they linger on the surface, due to cold weather and surface breezes that bunch or clump them up together during emergence. Later, when adults return from their mating swarm (along streamside) there is only sporadic feeding on ovipositors.

Trout seldom get excited over these slow-motion midges like they do caddis, but instead get very, very serious and focused showing lots of consistent, easy, slow rising as the pupae emerge and gather in the surface film. Look for smooth, slow, horizontal, showy noses and then dorsal fin and tail rise-form as trout, often gulping large numbers at a time, feed on midges. The best of surface midge fishing most frequently happens in slow or still water.

The stages and actions of caddis and midges, like mayflies and stoneflies, are easy to imitate once you can identify each. The graphic I've drawn should help make that simpler. Caddis are probably the easiest of all the main aquatic insects to tackle for imitation and to fish. They are great fun and, *trout love them*. Midges are on the opposite end of the spectrum. They require finely tuned, finesse fly tackle, long delicate leaders and tippets, and the most precisely accurate cast and perfect, drag-free-drift fly action for consistent success. But your rewards are some of the best in trout angling, in my opinion.

DAMSELFLIES AND DRAGONFLIES

amselflies and dragonflies, members of the order Odonata, are both important aquatic insect trout foods, especially in still waters and slow-moving streams. The adults are easy to see and identify, being generally large, beautifully colored, and with distinctive big heads and eyes. I've no doubt that most of you, from childhood on, have watched and been fascinated by the amazing acrobatics and hypnotic beauty of damsel and dragonflies.

Trout, particularly the larger wild ones, seem very fond of capturing and eating Odonata, both as the aquatic nymphs and the swift-flying adults. Looking back, I can say that many of the really large trout I've been fortunate enough to catch in still waters have been on imitations of damselfly and dragonfly nymphs.

Damselflies (Zygoptera)

Damselflies, true to their descriptive name, are the smaller and more delicate of the two suborders of Odonata, and as adults they are often spectacularly colored in electric blues and greens, ruby reds, and shiny jet-black. At rest, the adults hold their wings straight up and together, while dragonflies hold their wings straight out from their bodies. Damselflies are perhaps a more significant food for trout than dragonflies, due to the sheer large numbers of them inhabiting most trout waters. They are most abundant in those shallow, clear, still waters that have lush aquatic vegetation growing up to the surface. Other prime damselfly habitats include sloughs, spring creeks, marshes, and the slower-section margins of freestone streams, and rivers.

Damselflies, like dragonflies, have two life-cycle forms: the aquatic nymph and the "terrestrial" adult. Depending on the species, the life cycle varies as to the amount of time spent as a nymph and an adult, and in general damsels live underwater as the nymph form for one to two years and then as adults for several weeks to several months, actively feeding on other insects and mating. The nymphs emerge into adults most commonly during mid-spring to early summer, but this may occur even into early fall. Because emergence is a slow process, damsel (and dragon) nymphs must crawl up and out of the water, onto and up vertical structures, usually plants, rather than transform at the surface of the water as many other aquatic insects do. It is at this time that trout will feed

HOW TO IDENTIFY DAMSELFLIES AND DRAGONFLIES

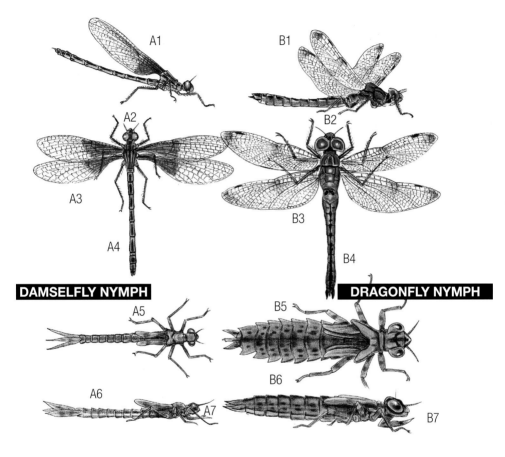

DAMSELFLY NYMPH

DRAGONFLY NYMPH

A1: Damselfly at rest: Both pairs of large wings are held upright and tightly together.

B1: Dragonfly at rest: Individual pairs of wings held apart and straight out from the thorax.

A2: Damselfly head: Has two large eyes and a very small pair of visible antennae.

B2: Dragonfly head: Has two very large compound eyes and a very small pair of visible antennae.

A3: Damselfly wings in flight: Wings are shorter than body, base of wings are yoked, and both pair are approximately the same size.

B3: Dragonfly wings in flight: Wings are shorter than the body and strongly veined. Second pair is wider than the first.

A4: Damselfly abdomen: Very slender and round, vividly segmented with no visible tail appendages.

B4: Dragonfly abdomen: Much thicker than damselfly and no distinguishable tail parts.

A5: Top view of damselfly nymph.

B5: Top view of dragonfly nymph.

A6: Damselfly nymph body: Overall appears to be slender and distinctly segmented with spidery legs and three large, paddle-like tail appendages.

B6: Dragonfly nymph body: Much wider and more robust than the damselfly with a triangular abdomen and no distinguishable tail parts.

A7: Damselfly nymph head: Two large eyes, small antennae, and labium tucked under the head.

B7: Dragonfly nymph head: Very large with large eyes, small antennae, and very large labium protruding below head.

NOTE: These illustrations depict the general shape, proportions, and colors of adult and nymph damselflies and dragonflies. Shapes, sizes, and color patterns vary considerably between species.

most heavily on crawling nymphs and frail young adults if they fall from their lofty perch. When the adults obtain their full flight-strength and vivid coloration, they are strong fliers and fierce small-insect predators. Trout most often eat the fully mature adults when the coupled, mating pairs return to the water to lay their eggs on the surface vegetation.

Damsel nymphs have a streamlined shape, are usually olive or tan colored, and have three wide, distinctive, paddle-like tail parts. Many species swim much like tiny fish and may even be mistaken for small, active minnows. Trout seem very attracted to these graceful swimmers and will take your damsel nymph fly with a quick rush!

Trout will also snatch newly emerged, frail adults as they try their wings on their first weak, solo flutter, low over the water. Look for swirls or splashes near surface vegetation. If you see trout leaping clear out of the water in good Odonata habitat, tie on an adult damselfly or dragonfly imitation quick, because they are most likely eating these active adult insects as they zoom near the water.

Dragonflies (Anisoptera)

Dragonflies are large, robust, fierce-looking aquatic insects that are ferocious predators and can even be quite cannibalistic. These facts, along with the huge size that some dragonflies attain, contributes to their other common names, such as "devil's darning needle," "horse stinger," and "mosquito hawk." At the same time, the graceful, colorful, unique shape of the adult dragonfly has become a very popular symbol on clothing, jewelry, and home furnishings in recent years.

Because of their size, abundance, and long life, they are favored foods for trout. Fortunately they are easy to imitate, and dragonfly nymph imitations are noted for their effectiveness in attracting large trout. With long, wide bodies and large heads with big eyes and long, spidery legs, they crawl, creep, and swim to catch their prey, impaling insects, leeches, and even small fish with a quick thrust of a spear-like, prehensile mouth part.

The forward propulsion of their unique swimming form comes from quickly expelling water that has been sucked into the end of the abdomen and through the internal gills. They make a quick, one- or two-inch-long darting movement with each expulsion—an action that you'll want to emulate with your dragonfly-nymph imitation for consistent results.

Dragon and damsel nymph flies are most effectively fished with a clear, intermediate fly line such as Scientific Anglers Stillwater. Present the nymphs over aquatic vegetation beds and allow them to sink just above the vegetation and slowly strip swim them in.

After living as a nymph for one to two years, the dragonfly adult emergence begins when the nymph contacts and crawls up a vertical object that protrudes out of the water or the first vertical object reached on dry land. The nymph will crawl fairly high, if possible, so that its maiden flight will be easier, and then laboriously splits its skin and emerges into its adult form. This will take at least an hour and sometimes much more. Eventually the pale tan or olive colored young adult takes its first, feeble flight, frequently ending in a watery disaster or capture by a bird, fish, frog, or another adult dragonfly!

This is the best adult phase to imitate, using an extended-bodied, spent-wing fly, especially if you see trout leaping out of the water in these marginal areas. When you cast, be ready and focused, because your fly may be taken "on the wing" as readily as the real thing! Those adults that survive their first 12 to 24 hours take on wonderfully brilliant colors, fantastic flight capabilities, and awesome predatory behavior on other insects like mosquitoes, midges, black flies, mayflies, damselflies, etc. Feeding and mating may continue for several weeks or months.

Damselflies and dragonflies are a real favorite of mine. They are easy to locate and identify, and few aquatic insects are more important to imitate when trout fishing in slow and still waters for those large, hungry trout.

HELLGRAMMITES

Megaloptera, the order name of hellgrammites or dobsonflies, is a name that could trigger anyone into thinking of large, scary creatures. And actually, hellgrammites do seem frightening when you first see or touch one. However, big fish—especially trout, smallmouth bass, sunfish, channel catfish, drum, and carp—see them only as big and delicious foods that have a high pain-to-gain food ratio like crayfish, but are well worth it. Because of their pinching mandibles and many animated legs, picking up and holding a live 3- or 4-inch hellgrammite larva instills a natural fear in most folks similar to holding a scorpion, crayfish, or tarantula. The dobsonfly, the flying adult stage, is one of the largest mature aquatic insects in North America and is no less ferocious-looking but, in reality, is harmless. I used to bait fish in my teens and twenties with ultra-light spin tackle or fly rods in the Ozarks and Smoky Mountains and, when I could get them, hellgrammites were second-to-none my favorite stream and river live bait.

Dobsonfly larvae are predators on aquatic insects. This one has just captured an emerging caddis pupa as a big brown zeros in on his own meal.

The hellgrammite is the larval form of the dobsonfly. Hellgrammites dwell in abundance in highly oxygenated gradient rubble and aquatic vegetation in clear, free-stone streams, rarely residing in ponds and lakes. They are aquatic larvae for two to four years before they mature and crawl out of the stream to pupate in damp, soft streamside soil or damp decaying terrestrial vegetation. The short-lived adults emerge, mate nearby, and lay their 2- to 3-inch white clusters of eggs over water on tree leaves, culverts or bridge abutments. When the eggs hatch, the larvae fall into the stream to begin their two- to four-year immature stage on and in the bottom structure.

Hellgrammite larvae are very aggressive predators on other aquatic insects, each other, and even small fish and crayfish. The large adults have

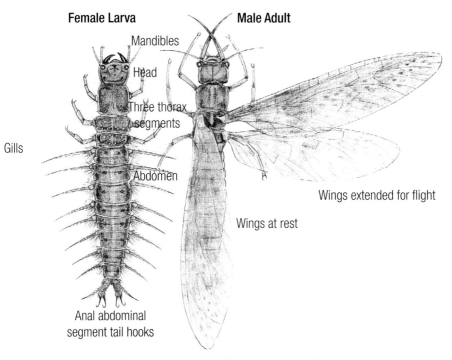

Female Larva

Mandibles

Head

Three thorax segments

Gills

Abdomen

Anal abdominal segment tail hooks

Male Adult

Wings extended for flight

Wings at rest

Hellgrammite/dobsonfly larva and adult.

even more impressive mandibles than the larva but they only use them for mating or biting intruders. I've most often observed the nocturnally active mega-winged Megaloptera adults at night on doors, walls, screen windows, and water-side docks in lighted areas. The adults are occasionally eaten by trout at night but it's the larvae that trout concentrate on day and night.

Larvae hide themselves on the sides and beneath rocks, burrow into the bottom gravel, or dwell in mats of live and dead vegetation. They are often mistaken by investigating fly fishers for stonefly nymphs, dragonfly nymphs, or predacious water-beetle larva. You can tell hellgrammite larvae from look-alikes by their lack of large head antenna, their large heavy mandibles, eight spiky pairs of gill filaments on their long leathery

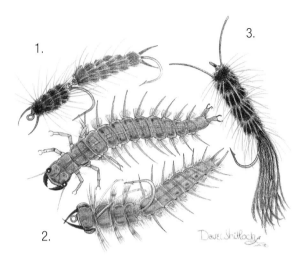

1. Woody's articulated hellgrammite
2. Whitlock's articulated hellgrammite
3. Murray's hellgrammite

abdomen, and a pair of sharply hooked anal pro-legs on their last abdominal segment. Oh, yes, and by their "skunky" odor.

Hellgrammites crawl over the stream bottom. When dislodged, they swim with an up-and-down motion of their long body, but usually only for short distances until they can regain their footing and secure themselves to or near the bottom again. So to best imitate them to catch a wise ol' trout, your fly should be fished *slowly* on or very close to the stream bottom. The ideal hellgrammite fly should have a large, slender, dark profile and soft leathery feel and have an articulated form. It should sink rapidly and swim or crawl with the hook point up and have a hook snag guard. The color should be a dark, dirty blend of brown, black, and olive. Some popular hellgrammite flies are Murray's Hellgrammite, Whitlock's Hellgrammite,

Woody's Hellgrammite, O'Hellgy's Hellgrammite, and Kauffman's Black Stone Nymph.

Fishflies, in the subfamily Chauliodinae, are very similar in both the larval and adult forms to dobsonflies, subfamily Corydalinae, and thus may be confused with them. However, it probably is not a significant error as imitating them with hellgrammite flies or vice-versa makes little difference to a trout!

I prefer to fish this imitation with either a floating line and long leader or a number III or IV sink rate, 4-foot sink tip and a 5-foot leader. Either of these choices gives you good fly drift-and-drag control as well as sensitive strike detection in streams and rivers. Usually the take is telegraphed by a sudden stop or hard jerk because big trout and other game fish love these critters and capture the real larva with an eager force.

It's safe to say no hellgrammite larva ever won a beauty contest or became anyone's pet. But sizeable larvae are available year-round and they are eagerly devoured by most predatory, freshwater game fish. Seining a few to get a good look at them, then trying to tie your own pattern or buying good imitations and fishing them like the real thing gives you a sure edge over many of the smaller food simulations most often used for catching those bigger trout.

BACKSWIMMERS AND WATER BOATMEN

Focus your gaze just below the water surface right along the shallow shoreline of a pond, river slough, or slow-moving spring creek, and you'll most likely notice one or two members of the Hemiptera order—the water bugs. Called "backswimmers" or "water boatmen," you'll see them erratically rowing about, surfacing to breathe and diving again. Trout living there also notice these two unusual aquatic bugs and frequently dine on them. To take a closer look at these unique little water bugs, simply make a swipe or two with a small aquarium net to capture several. Once they are in the net and removed from the water, they'll begin a popcorn-like series of jumps or will take to wing and fly away to the water, dive into it, and disappear!

Both bugs are small, have a streamlined, beetle-like form, and one or two pairs of long oar-like legs. Put them quickly into a container of clear water and they'll display their large oar-like legs. The ones swimming

Water boatmen and backswimmers are extremely plentiful and widely distributed in ponds, spring creeks, sloughs, and slow sections of trout streams, similar to water bugs. Trout readily feed on them year-round.

upside down most of the time are, of course, the backswimmers. The water boatmen swim back up and appear to have a distinctively silvery veil over their entire bodies and legs. This is because the water boatman is completely covered, and the backswimmer partially so, with a unique velvety pile that traps a thin film of air next to their bodies when beneath the water, causing a silvery sheen. The trapped air is used for breathing and buoyancy. Because of this buoyancy, they will slowly rise to the surface unless they continuously swim or cling to watery structures.

Both insects have one or more generations per year and the adults over-winter, even under ice. Their metamorphosis is simple: egg, nymph, and adult. Nymphs undergo five instars from egg to adult. It's common to

BACKSWIMMERS AND WATER BOATMEN

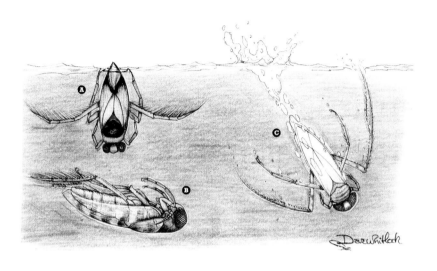

A. At the water's surface, backswimmers breathe air through an abdominal air port.

B. Backswimmers are easily distinguished from water boatmen because the former swim on their backs.

C. Water boatmen frequently surface, fly, and dive beneath the surface. An envelope of silvery air clings to their bodies as they dive and swim.

have several sizes of nymphs and adults sharing the same water. I'd suggest that the larger, more colorful adults might be the better form of imitation to interest trout, which seem to cruise along and opportunistically feed on them. Before I knew about these neat little water bugs, I'd often notice small insects erratically flying over the water then diving into it with a small, but detectable, *plop!* These are the adults during mating, relocation flights, or air intake. If you notice this activity, it's a good clue to consider using a backswimmer or water boatman imitation, especially in beaver

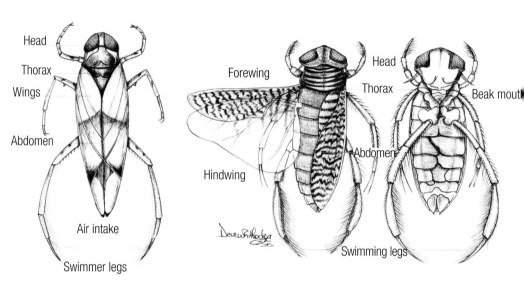

Head
Thorax
Wings
Abdomen
Air intake
Swimmer legs

Forewing
Hindwing
Head
Thorax
Abdomen
Beak mouth
Swimming legs

Backswimmer and water boatman anatomy.

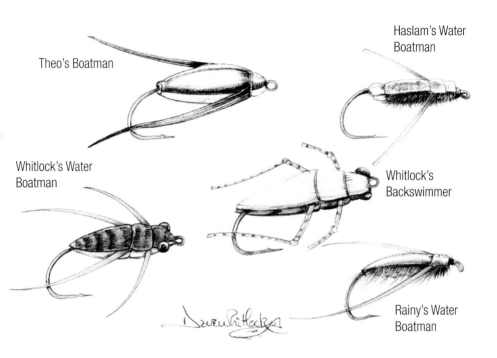

Theo's Boatman

Haslam's Water Boatman

Whitlock's Water Boatman

Whitlock's Backswimmer

Rainy's Water Boatman

Water boatman and backswimmer imitations.

ponds or backwaters of spring creeks. If you stomach-pump trout you hook in ponds, lagoons, sloughs, and slow streams, they'll often be packed tight with either or both bugs.

These little bugs are about 8 to 15 millimeters and are available year-round. You'll find good times to fish them are from early spring to late fall. I'd recommend using a floating or a clear Stillwater intermediate line, 7½- to 9-foot knotless nylon tipped with 24 to 30 inches of 4x or 5x fluorocarbon tippet.

If you can spot cruising trout, cast well ahead of them with the floating line setup, allow several seconds for the fly to sink to the level at which the trout are cruising or near the bottom. Then, as the fish approaches, begin a series of moderately slow one-inch-long line strips to cause the bug to swim upward, imitating the characteristic rowing-motion swim toward the surface.

When there are no visible trout to cast to, I prefer the clear intermediate line set up. It allows me to search more water per retrieve without spooking fish it passes over.

One of my fondest successes with these bugs was on a big slough off Idaho's Silver Creek. A number of 18- to 25-inch rainbows were making individual circuits of the slough, taking water boatmen and scuds. I'd spot one, cast well ahead of it, then as the trout got close to the fly, I'd lift the imitation and begin to slow strip it toward the surface. These big, well-educated, Silver Creek trophies would speed up, then brake speed, open a white mouth and suck in my flies . . . and the duel would be on. Most of the fish I hooked that day were too much for the tippet size, aquatic vegetation, and my skills, but I did land a couple that were well over 20 inches.

To imitate these little bugs, I use Swiss straw for their bodies and strands of the smallest variegated or banned rubber strands or small, thin, goose biots for their long, oar-like middle or rear legs. Their backs should be black or at least a dark color, and their bellies a white or cream. For the silvery sheen, a strip of thin poly-bag or pearlescent mylar laid over or wrapped over the body does nicely. Glass or metallic beads are also useful for making imitations and size 16 and 14 weighted hooks are best. Be sure if you are specifically imitating the backswimmer that you tie your imitation light side on top of the book's shank. What self-respecting trout would eat one any other way?

Water boatmen are among the most plentiful and widely distributed aquatic insects in the world. They live in fresh, brackish, and salt water and at all altitudes from Death Valley to 15,000 feet. They are even more favored by other fish such as perch, crappie, bass, and bluegill. I've even observed them in swimming pools, barrels of cistern water, and septic lagoons.

If this season or next you have plans to fish beaver ponds, shallow sloughs off streams, or slow-flowing spring creeks, along with some scuds, leeches, damselfly nymphs, and midges, include some water boatmen or backswimmer bugs in your fly box for the best possible success in these waters.

THREE

Minnows

Minnows I

rout feed on three principal food forms: insects, minnows, and crustaceans. I discussed the basic groups of aquatic insects that are most important to trout and trout anglers earlier. Now let's cover the forage minnows and minnow-like small fish that are so often on a trout's menu.

"Minnow" is a common term used by fly fishers, generally referring to the very small fish that reside in our North American trout waters. Although all sizes of trout eat them, generally larger trout, as they increase in size and age, switch from aquatic insects to larger morsels, particularly minnows and other small fish, including their own kind . . . even their own offspring!

I'm always amused when someone tells me that brown trout or bull trout are terrible cannibals that eat other trout such as rainbows, brook trout, or cutthroats. *All* trout, and most salmon, are cannibals. I once hatched approximately 500 each of browns, rainbow, brooks, cutthroats, silver, and king salmon eggs in a huge, stream-like aquarium to study them. Even though they had ample live shrimp to eat, they all ate each other. Eventually the silvers and kings won out, eliminating all but a few of even their own kind before I finished the study.

In order to simplify the huge array of minnows for my book, *Aquatic Trout Foods,* I grouped them into three categories according to their shapes, colors, water-column positions, and schooling habits, as well as how each had evolved to fit a particular type of environment. Here are those groups:

Group I: Open water (lakes and big rivers); live in the water column and not on the bottom; silvery-colored big-school minnows like threadfin shad, smelt, alewife, and silver sides.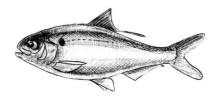

Group II: Narrow waters (like streams); colorful-sided, loosely schooled minnows like dace, chubs, shiners, stickle-back, and small trout.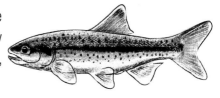

Group III: Bottom-dwelling; drab colored with mottled back and sides; solitary or small-colony minnows like sculpins, darters, mad-tom catfish, and sucker minnows.

GROUP I

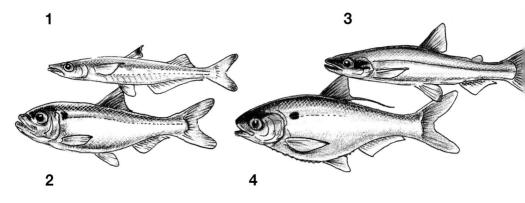

1. Brook Silverside
2. Alewife
3. Rainbow Smelt
4. Gizzard Shad

Group I

I'll start with Group I minnows. These small fish most frequently live in the wide-open water expanses of larger ponds, lakes, estuaries, and large rivers. Some will temporarily migrate into smaller creeks to spawn in the spring, but, for the most part, they are large-water dwellers. Their coloring plays an important protective role. When viewed from above, the backs of this type of minnow are the same color as the water, providing significant camouflage from overhead predators, while the highly reflective metallic tints of silver or bright pale gold on their sides help them remain invisible to underwater predators. This is a form of mirror camouflage. Even adult trout, char, and salmon living in large, open-water expanses adopt this very effective mirror camo.

Generally, predator fish will follow schools of Group I minnows as they move around in their daily foraging. Over deep water, these minnows will often form massive, tight schools to help each other detect predators and to discourage or confuse those predators by the huge size and actions of the school. Most of these little fish are plankton feeders, so all of them can efficiently forage in open waters. The alewife of the Great Lakes are one of the most typical Group I minnows.

To catch trout, char, and salmon that are foraging on schools of Group I minnows swimming in deep water, you can learn to use fish locators to find minnows. Often, especially early morning and late afternoon on calm days, these same schools can be found foraging at the surface or are chased there by predators such as cormorants, loons, and large fish. If you watch closely, you'll find that diving gulls and terns are great high-flying signals of this surface activity and, often, you can see their feeding activity from up to a mile away.

Tailwater rivers, especially during high hydroelectric generation in the winter and early spring periods, make hot spots for Group I minnows, like threadfin shad and smelt. A long, deep, cold spell can thermally shock these minnows, making them too lethargic to swim effectively, which then allows them to pass helplessly through generators from the

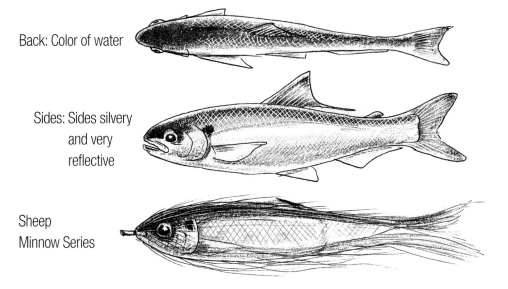

Back: Color of water

Sides: Sides silvery and very reflective

Sheep Minnow Series

lake to the river. Millions of these minnows may be set adrift each day down the river, and opportunistic tailwater trout and salmon simply devour them.

Streamers that match the Group I shape and color patterns should be carefully fished with actions that mostly imitate a crippled and dying minnow. So, you don't want to *over retrieve* these streamers. A fluttering, slow-sinking, or surface v-waking imitation is usually the best fly design. About fifteen years ago, I designed a Group I streamer, the Sheep Minnow, so I could make this sort of opportunity really productive.

Here's a tip: If the water is clear and the surface calm, I've found that using a Scientific Anglers (clear) Stillwater Fly Line is amazingly effective because you can cast and strip your line over fish, usually without spooking them.

When the minnow schools are deeper, it's necessary to use a uniform sinking fly line with a number-four or -five sink rate. Trolling isn't for everyone, but it is a very efficient way to get and keep flies and lures in these deeper zones, where the schools of Group I minnows are often holding.

When I designed the Sheep Minnow series, one thing I discovered was the importance of concealing the hook bend and point. This is necessary because Group I minnows are usually in very clear water and imitations are often best fished slowly. Trout and salmon get a good, long, clear look at the fly. To make the fly hook harder to see, I use a highly reflective, nickel-plated hook.

Another critical property of a good Group I imitation is that it has the natural profile and action of a minnow fluttering, struggling, and sinking. A lot of streamers only look good when they are being moved rapidly forward. When stopped or fished slowly, the heavier hook bend sinks, while the lighter back and body materials float, causing the fly and hook to separate and lose its form. To prevent this problem with my Sheep Minnow, I tie more hair on the bottom and balance the weight of the hook with lead wire so that the hook bend weight is the same as the head weight.

Trout and salmon often school up to forage on these Group I minnows. The smaller fish tend to do most of the school bashing, while larger fish remain beneath the melee to pick up the easier-to-catch, disabled, sinking minnows. Try to let your imitation sink deeper, and fish it with the least amount of action to zero in on these larger fish.

Smaller trout often chase and kill Group I minnows at the surface, but larger trout remain deeper to pick off crippled minnows as they sink.

Minnows II

The most common forage minnows for stream trout are the Group II minnows. They have the classic minnow shape and, often, colorfully marked bodies and fins that help them to blend with the color of the water and bottom structures in the stream. These minnows form loose schools or small groups for protection and are agile, quick swimmers that mainly feed on tiny insects and crustaceans from the surface down through the water column. Group II minnows are quite trout-like in their swimming behavior, preferring the shallow sides of riffles, runs, flats, and tails of pool. It's not uncommon to catch them while fishing dry flies and nymphs. Most spawn in the spring or early summer and many species at that time, males especially, become vividly colorful on their fins and sides with brilliant glowing yellows, golds, and crimson reds. Within some species, the spawning males will develop a number of small, horny projections on their heads and backs. Locals often call them "horny head minnows" or "chubs."

Some good examples of Group II minnows are blacknose dace, creek chubs, and redbelly shiners. Compared to Group I minnows, Group II minnows are more torpedo-shaped, colorful, and less reflective.

EXAMPLES OF GROUP II

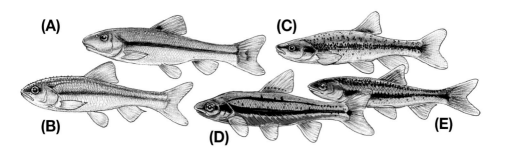

(A) Creek Chub
(B) Common Shiner—male in spawning colors
(C) Blacknose Dace
(D) Redbelly Dace—male in spawning colors
(E) Rainbow Shiner

Larger trout, char, and landlocked salmon feed fairly regularly on Group II minnows, but because these minnows have more speed and agility than the tightly schooled, open-water Group I minnows, conditions have to be right for predators to catch them. Three of these conditions are: higher water levels, which prevent minnows from taking shelter in the shallows; low-light or storms, when trout feel safer about leaving their cover and chasing them; and heavy minnow spawning activity. Trout also have an excellent opportunity to feed when these Group II minnows are distracted with their own feeding and any time a minnow becomes sick or disabled and cannot swim with the school. Trout hold much tighter when light is bright and water is low and very clear. At that time, nymphing is the better choice.

GROUP II MINNOWS AND IMITATIONS

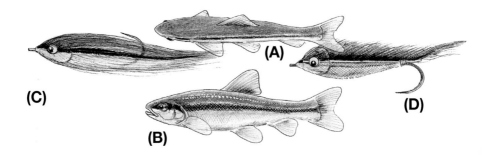

(A) Top View   (C) Sheep Minnow Swimmer Fly
(B) Side View   (D) Zonker Minnow Fly

Last spring, I witnessed some bizarre minnow predation by several nice rainbow trout in a Missouri spring creek. A large group of brilliant cardinal shiners had constructed a large gravel mound and were busy laying and fertilizing eggs over it. These trout would slowly swim to the mounds, lay quietly as the minnows returned to their activity, and simply suck one in every minute or so until they had their fill.

Larger fish can swim faster than a similar small fish, so the smaller, slower minnows survive trout pressure by using nimble maneuverability, taking advantage of quick access to shallow water and leaping out of the water or diving into or under stream plants or structures.

A good time to choose Group II minnow imitations is when you want to catch larger trout, especially if there are no apparent hatches or plentiful crustaceans. Try to begin with a mindset that you will be triggering a predator's basic instinct to attack a *vulnerable* creature.

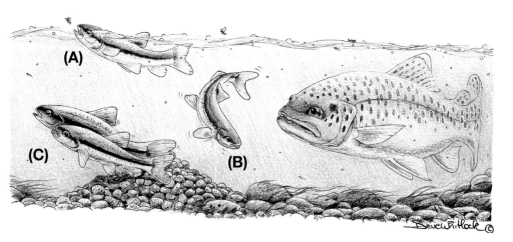

GROUP II TROUT FEEDING OPPORTUNITIES

(A) When minnows feed—especially at the surface
(B) When minnows are in distress
(C) When minnows are on spawn run or actively spawning

First, observe which minnows are present, and then pick a streamer that imitates the minnow's size, shape, and color. Present your streamer to suggest ultimate vulnerability. If possible, swim the fly sideways to the current, close to the nose of a trout, char, or salmon or give it erratic movements that depict helplessness, panic, or a dying action. Longer casts cover more water and give following trout a longer time to take the fly before they see you.

When water is shallow (from one to four feet deep) a floating or short sink-tip line will fish Group II streamers ideally. In very clear water, try a colorless Scientific Anglers Stillwater line. It's deadly for long retrieves. When the water is deeper, you'll catch more and larger trout by using No. IV or V sink-rate, uniform-sinking lines and swimming the streamer near the bottom.

Most Group II minnows have a tricolor pattern. They have a dark back, usually some shade of olive, golden olive, golden or brown; their sides often have a dark horizontal stripe from nose to tail; and their lower sides and belly will be a pearly yellow, cream, or white. Their fins are also often a colorful yellow, gold-orange, or red. They have medium-sized eyes which are not as vivid as the Group I minnows. I like to use tying materials for the backs and tails that absorb water quickly and have a lot of swimming action in the water. Marabou, soft-webbed cock hackle, fox, or rabbit fur Zonker strips, and flashabou or flashabou accent are my favorite Group II streamer tying materials. Metallic or pearly-braided Mylar tubing and soft white or cream-colored dubbing make great Group II minnow bellies.

Classic streamer designs for Group II minnows are Zonkers, Matuka Minnows, Swimmer Sheep Minnows, and Thunder Creek Minnows. Clouser minnows are excellent too, if the eyes aren't too large, so as to allow the fly to swim instead of sink and jig. Many of the classic Maine bucktail and hackled trolling streamers are excellent as well.

Identifying and matching Group II minnows will add more spice, dimension, and depth to your trout fly fishing and most likely more and much larger trout as well.

Minnows III

Nature always amazes me with its ability to evolve species to fit perfectly into every conceivable niche on this planet. One of the most interesting examples is that niche that exists on the bottom of a trout stream. The group of minnows that inhabit this area—sculpins, darters, madtom catfish and certain suckers—are small fish that are so specialized for streambed life that they don't remotely resemble the Group I and II minnows that I discussed in the last two chapters. They've evolved to crawl or dart from rock to rock and are almost invisible to a predator's eye because they are as skillful with camouflage as a chameleon. Foraging for food is by either ambush or methodic, careful moves from place to place. Every trout stream I've studied in North and South America, Europe, and New Zealand has various forms of these Group III minnows.

If there's a fault in their adaptation, it's their lack of ability to swim quickly for any significant distance, and so trout can easily run them down once these minnows are flushed from bottom-structure hideaways. This is why the larger trout prefer to feed on them over the speedy Group I and II minnows. It's been my experience that imitating Group III is the surest consistent way to catch trophy-size trout. Most of the avid big-trout *bait* fishers I've met use little else if sculpins are available.

Group III minnows have backs, sides, and fins that are drab-colored and mottled to imitate the bottom structure of the stream on which they rest, and their body, fin shapes, and density are all engineered for living on and moving over the bottom. Because of the way their heads and backs are sloped and their bodies quickly taper back, moving water causes them to plane downward, holding them securely to the bottom even in the swiftest current flows. Reduced pelvic and caudal fills allow these little fish to fit flat along the stream bottom while their pectoral fins are large and extended and are actually used to crawl along like little underwater lizards. A further adaptation in some of this group is the absence of an air or swim bladder which means that, although they can swim, they can't hold in the water column and immediately sink as soon as they stop swimming. The advantage to this is that it allows them to be consistently heavier than water so they can live a more efficient, bottom-dwelling lifestyle.

Most Group III minnows feed by simply sitting patiently on the bottom and allowing their prey to approach them, much like a frog or toad would feed on insects. Their menu consists largely of aquatic-insect nymphs and larvae, aquatic worms, scuds, sowbugs, snails, fish eggs, and other fish fry, as well as some aquatic plants and dead aquatic creatures. Sculpins and madtoms are notorious for pulling bait-fishers' worms or egg-baited hooks into rock crevices, hanging them up and stealing the bait. Occasionally, while trout fishing, I've *unintentionally* caught big sculpins on nymphs, San Juan worms, and egg flies drifted close to the bottom.

EXAMPLES OF GROUP III

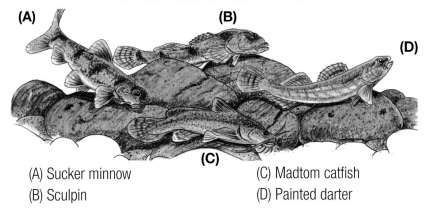

(A) **(B)** **(D)**

(C)

(A) Sucker minnow   (C) Madtom catfish
(B) Sculpin   (D) Painted darter

The most bizarre experience I can remember, related to catching sculpins, happened on the Arkansas Norfork River just below Norfork Dam. While fishing there, I met a man who said he was "fly fishing for sculpins!" That fascinated me, so I watched as he jigged a size 20, half-inch-long, red San Juan worm using two feet of monofilament line attached to an old fly-rod tip between some large, river-side rocks. He caught several three- to four-inch sculpins and immediately put each in an icebox. He told me that he sold them to a nearby trout-fishing resort for 25 cents a piece. Creatures might adapt to every niche, but humans can always find a way to make money from every niche.

Group III fish are among the most environmentally sensitive and are the first to die off if the trout stream develops dissolved oxygen or chemical pollution problems. If you observe more than an occasional dead or sick Group III minnow, or if they all seem too disappear from your stream, call your local fish and game department and report your observation as soon as possible. Collect the dead ones and freeze or refrigerate them for the investigating biologist. If these minnows can't survive, it's very possible that your resident trout may soon be perishing, too.

Big trout will feed on Group III minnows all year, especially when the water level is normal or slightly high. Low-light levels are best, such

GROUP III MINNOWS AND IMITATIONS

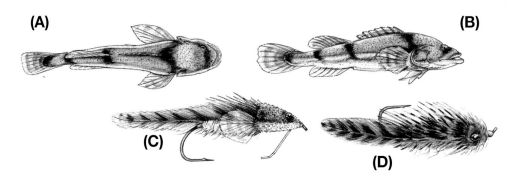

(A) Sculpin minnow—top view   (B) Sculpin minnow—side view
(C) Matuka Sculpin (with Snag Guard)   (D) Near Nuff Sculpin

as at dawn and dust, all night, and on heavily overcast, stormy days. Good areas to fish are the deeper riffles, runs, and tail-outs that have coarse-rock bottoms or considerable aquatic-vegetation beds. Rig up a 5- to 10-foot-long, uniform sink-tip line with a 3- to 4-foot leader. Then try drifting in a boat with the stream's current near the shoreline and casting your imitation minnow tight against the bank structure of the deeper riffle and runs. Large trout hold just outside the shallows waiting to gobble down minnows that are flushed out by herons, mink, cormorants, mergansers, or wading livestock. But don't waste time on long retrievals because usually, if it's *gonna* happen, the take will be quick and very visual just as the streamer slips into the deeper, colored water.

I've had my most consistent success catching the really big trout at night. I use a large, 4- to 8-inch-long, bulky, solid-black Matuka sculpin fished on a floating line with a 10-foot OX leader and over very shallow water. The big Matuka sculpin, slowly retrieved just under the surface,

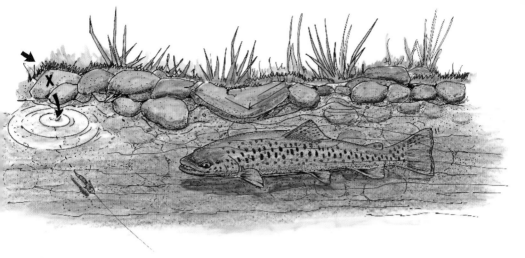

With a short sink-tip line, use an off-the-bank method of presenting Group III imitations to trout holding in the first colored water near the shoreline.

creates a strong V-wake that really attracts those huge night-feeders. This method also avoids those aggravating bottom hang-ups and you can usually see and hear the strikes, which are often nothing less than terrifying in the dark.

The most consistent way I've found to find and catch big trout during brighter conditions is to use a Group III imitation with a IV- or V-rate, uniform-sinking line, and a 3- to 4-foot leader. Using this combo, you can crawl or dart the streamer (tied with a snag guard) right along the bottom in the deeper water where the larger fish hang out in the daytime.

In my lifetime, there has been a continuous evolution of Group III imitations. The first I recall was Don Gapen's Muddler Minnow, followed by Troth's Bullhead, William's Spuddler, my Matuka Sculpin, Woolly Buggers, Woolhead Sculpins, and Partridge Sculpins, as well as my Near Nuff Sculpin . . . and each of these is time-proven effective. I prefer the Matuka Sculpin when a precise imitation is needed for the largest and most selective trout and char. When I fish for less selective or relatively smaller trout that are eating sculpins, darters, or madtoms, my easy-to-tie Near Nuff Sculpin is the choice.

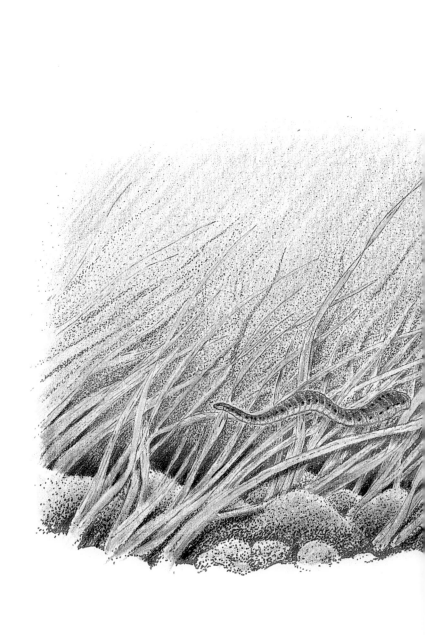

FOUR

Crustaceans and Annelids

SCUDS

In many trout fisheries, crustaceans are a very important food form. In fact, because they offer the richest food value for the least forage effort or energy output, trout often rely on crustaceans as much as aquatic insects or minnows on a day-to-day basis. These aquatic invertebrates include the freshwater species of shrimp, scuds, sowbugs, crayfish, and pancora. In waters that have abundant crustacean life, trout are usually robust in body shape, grow very fast, are brilliantly colored outside, and have deep orange-colored flesh.

I always remember what Rip Collins told me regarding the 40-pound plus, record brown trout he caught in Arkansas's Little Red River tail water. He said its stomach contained two or three *pounds* of sowbugs and scuds! It's amazing that such a monster brown would eat such diminutive food, but these abundant, accessible, tiny crustaceans were one of the major reasons it had grown so large.

Scud (Amphipoda)

Scuds, which are often incorrectly called freshwater shrimp, are one of the most significant forms of freshwater crustaceans on which trout regularly dine. There are some 800 freshwater species, but the two genera that are the most important as trout food—and, by extension, as species for trout fishers to imitate—are hyalalla and gammarus.

Most species of scuds succeed best in trout waters that are enriched with calcium carbonate and have a pH factor 7 or higher. They, like insects, need the calcium carbonate to form the exoskeleton (their skin). Waters that originate from limestone substrates such as springs or that flow over limestone surfaces generally have the best population of scuds and other crustaceans, as well as good trout growth rates. Scuds eat both

(A) Scud   (B) Crayfish   (C) Freshwater Shrimp   (D) Sowbug

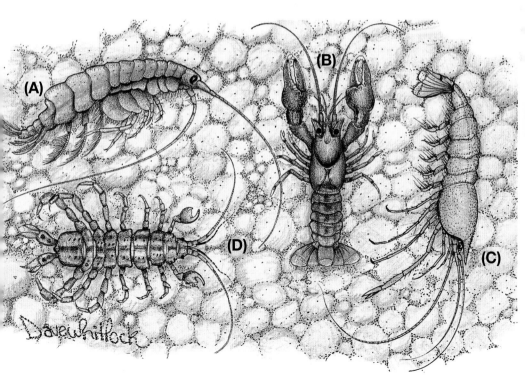

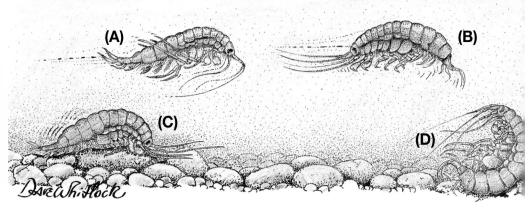

TROUT FEED ON SCUDS WHEN THEY ARE:

(A) Swimming forward
(B) Swimming backward
(C) Crawling
(D) Dead and tumbling in the current

plant and animal matter, preferring to live where there are abundant aquatic plants or rocks well-encrusted with algae or moss. It takes only a moment of investigation of these structures to detect whether scuds are present. They do well in aerated, unpolluted, flowing, as well as still waters. Scuds have a simple life cycle of egg to juvenile to adult that spans a few weeks to one or two years. They range in size, depending on species, from 1/16 inch to 1 inch, with the average being about 1/4 to 3/8 inch.

Scuds crawl or swim forward with their several, complex pairs of legs. They characteristically swim with sort of a jerky-zoom motion through the water in an irregular swimming movement right side up, on their sides and upside down. In some waters they are called back-swimmers because of these unusual swimming positions. When scuds crawl or swim, they have a more or less linear shape but when they are held captive in your hand or after they die, they form a "C" shape. Most scud imitations are tied on extra-short, curved hook shanks that imitate this "C" shape. To more precisely imitate free-swimming, living scuds, tie or buy imitations on straight hook shanks.

Scuds vary a lot in color depending on their species, diet, skin replacement cycle, and health. Most are a light dun-gray with tones of tan, olive, yellow, or orange. A few colonies I've seen are a definite pinkish orange and most scuds will take on a similar bright coloration after death. Consequently, the dead, pinkish-orange scuds you might discover in a trout's stomach were not necessarily that color when eaten alive by that trout.

There's a popular un-weighted, C-shaped, orange scud pattern, frequently used in tail waters, that is supposed to imitate scuds that die and dry out when the flow from the dam is decreased greatly, causing the water level to rapidly decline. The scuds, as well as many other aquatic food forms, often can't retreat fast enough and so may get beached out of the water and soon die. With the next rise in the water, these dead, sun-dried scuds drift downstream. Imitations are fly fished with a natural "dead drift" either on or under the surface.

Live scud imitations work best in flowing water when fished with a natural downstream drift and close to the bottom structures where scuds live. The use of highly visible, floating strike indicators on flowing waters, especially those waters that have windy or riffed surfaces, significantly animates the fly, enhancing trout interest, while making strike detection so much easier.

For still-water ponds, sloughs, and lakes, the most effective way to fish scud imitations is to present to an area with a long, 40- to 60-foot cast, using a #1 sinking line, and count the weighted scud down to a depth just over the top of the aquatic vegetation or the stream bottom. Then slowly retrieve with a "figure 8" line twist or use 1- to 3-inch-long, slow-paced line strips. The ultimate line for this is the clear Scientific Anglers WF/S Stillwater line. Because it is clear and sinks below, creating no wake by the line on the water surface, it allows the scud to be retrieved long distances, in still water, without surface wind drag and without scaring trout as it passes by or over. But because you cannot see this line in the water, you must detect the trout's take by feeling the change in line tension or sometimes the jerk of the strike. So, keep your rod tip pointed toward the fly and hold it at or just an inch or two above the water surface to avoid slack-line sag and to enhance your strike detection as well as hooking efficiency.

Scuds grace nearly every classic, blue-ribbon, spring-creek, and tailwater trout fishery, and alkaline ponds and lakes across North America. They, and crustaceans as a group, are in large part responsible for the great success of these waters. A few that come to my mind as favorites are: the tailwaters of the White River in Arkansas and Missouri; the Colorado River tailwater below Lake Powell; the Big Horn River below Yellowtail Dam; and Silver Creek and Henry's Lake in Idaho.

Good scuddin!

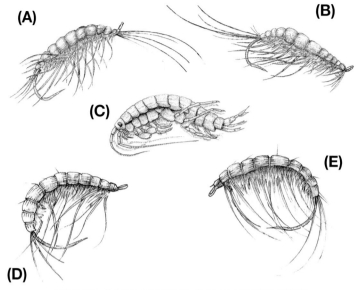

SCUD AND POPULAR IMITATIONS

(A) Forward-swimming scud fly—straight hook
(B) Back-swimming scud fly—straight hook
(C) Live swimming scud
(D) Scud fly tied on curved hook
(D) Sun-dried or dead scud on curved hook

AQUATIC SOWBUGS

The crustaceans we call sowbugs are second only to scuds as important trout food in many streams that have a higher alkaline content, such as spring creeks or freestone streams flowing over substantial limestone substrates. Our Ozark tailwaters are fantastic sowbug habitats. In general, sowbugs live in most waters that also support scuds and crayfish, and because they are a bit more tolerant of lower-quality water, can occur in some waters that are absent of scuds.

I guess someone named these neat little nocturnal creatures "sowbugs" because they crawl slowly and root over stream or pond bottoms, eating a diet that could be compared to a sow pig's: live and dead, terrestrial, and aquatic plants; insects and decaying aquatic animals. Other names for them that you might recognize are: cressbug, pillbug, and roly-poly bug. Although they might not have a very respectful or pretty-sounding name, trout and trout fly fishers who know about them have a pretty high opinion of these critters. There's even at least one festival held in their honor! It happens each spring in Mountain Home, Arkansas, and hundreds of fly fishers and fly tiers attend the fun-filled Sow-Bug Roundup.

My first recall of the incredible effectiveness of sowbug flies was years ago during a visit to meet and interview Pennsylvania's famous limestone spring-creek trio: Charley Fox, Ed Shenk, and Ed Koch. While I was fishing with Ed Koch on Falling Spring one day, he guided his simple, gray, muskrat-fur cressbug pattern straight downstream with a 6-foot rod and nothing more than his leader. As the little bug slipped right to the nose of one of several big trout that were holding beneath the underwater ledges . . . it promptly took his offering! Then he did it again and again. *I was amazed!*

Sowbugs have a compressed, eight-segmented body with seven pairs of legs that stick out to the sides of the first seven segments; two pairs of large, distinctive antennae; and one pair of flat, tail-like appendages. They can only crawl over and under bottom structures, and when dislodged from the bottom, they are seemingly helpless until they sink back to the bottom. They range in length from 5 to 25 millimeters or hook sizes 20 to 12. Size 16 and 18 seem to be the best average. I have seen a few Goliath specimens—in small, very rich spring creeks with few fish predators—that would take a size 8 hook to imitate! They tend to be a variable intensity of mottled, grayish color, with occasionally tan or olive overtones in some colonies. I recommend you seine a few from your waters and check their sizes and color. They do not turn pink or orange when dead, like scuds do.

Sowbugs have a simple life cycle of egg to immature sowbug to mature sowbug. There seem to be all sizes in a single colony, but there are more and larger ones through the warmer water months than in the winter. Because there are always adult-size naturals available, sowbug imitations are a good year-round fly choice to catch trout in waters where they occur. We used to tell newcomers of the sowbug-laden White River and Norfork River tailwaters that we had separate patterns for sowbug nymphs, emergers, duns, and spinners. We'd even give them a few duns and spinners, but eventually we always confessed the joke.

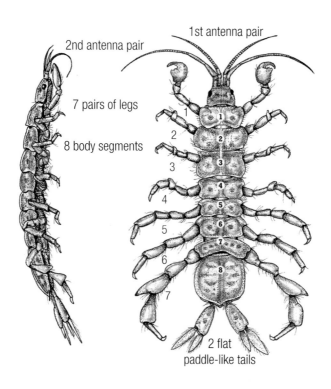

2nd antenna pair

1st antenna pair

7 pairs of legs

8 body segments

2 flat paddle-like tails

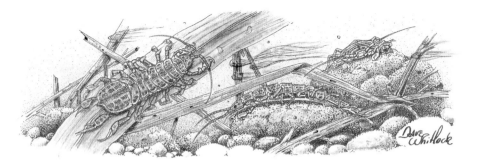

In their natural habitat, sowbugs crawl slowly over bottom structure to forage. Unlike scuds, they cannot swim.

Sowbug imitations are most effective when fished at a natural-drift speed and on *or very close to the bottom* of the stream. They are seldom effective in ponds and lakes because crawling a fly along the bottom is very difficult and inefficient. In streams, the flies are most effective when there is turbulence or quick water-level changes that tend to dislodge the naturals. For instance, not long ago, while drift fishing with sowbug imitations just below Bull Shoals Dam, I noticed a distinctive increase in hookups with the big rainbows and browns for a period of 20 to 30 minutes whenever one or more of the eight generators were turned on. It was obvious that these sudden surges of water were dislodging more sowbugs than when the flow was constant. Right at that time the trout would get very excited and feed much more aggressively.

The most productive way to present and fish sowbug imitations is with a floating line, floating leader, strike indicator, and a length of tippet that is as long or longer than the stream's depth. Make it longer by a third or half if the water speed is significantly swift, or tie it on equal

SOWBUG FLY

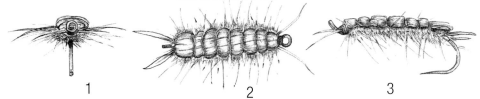

1
2
3

1. Front view
2. Dorsal view
3. Side view

to the depth if the water moves slowly. The sowbug imitation should be well weighted to get the fly down deep quickly. A small split shot or twist-on weight, 8 to 10 inches above the fly, can also greatly increase the trout hook-ups by getting the fly down to the bottom faster and holding it there better. If the indicator is occasionally showing that the fly or the weight is touching bottom, that's ideal!

Trout tend to take sowbugs slowly and subtly, so really focus and react to the slightest indicator change in speed, float, attitude, or submersion. Never think it's the bottom . . . *set every time it even looks guilty*. Remember, they can't swim and don't emerge so do all you can to get a natural, downstream drift. The larger, stream-savvy trout seem to have it figured out, and they don't chase a sowbug up or across stream or if it's moving downstream faster than the current speed. The most consistent and ideal depth and drift is accomplished with an upstream cast and presentation. Drag problems with across or downstream casts can quickly defeat the precise on-the-bottom, natural drift that is typical of sowbug activity.

There's a tributary creek called "Dry Run," that flows into the Norfork River just below Norfork Dam in Arkansas. Its main water source is the discharge from the Norfork Federal Trout Hatchery, which feeds several million immature trout every day. Dry Run Creek is heavily populated, *wall-to-wall,* with trophy-size rainbows, browns, and Snake River cutthroat, with from 5 to 25 pounds being common. One square foot of Dry Run's bottom will yield approximately 200 to 500 sowbugs! The hatchery's rich elixir of organic trout effluent feeds these tiny gray pigs, and all those monster trout hogs feed on them. Oh, I almost forgot to tell you: Dry Run is open only to public catch-and-release fishing and only if you are *under 16* or *ambulatory handicapped.*

Sowbugs are easy to imitate and to fish, and trout always seem to be willing to eat them year-round. Check your stream for them by seining or turning over several stones. If you find them present, *boy, you are in luck!* Good Sowbuggin!

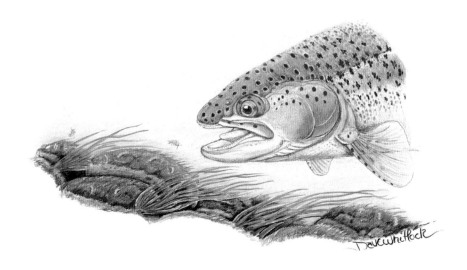

CRAYFISH

Crayfish are one of the most widely distributed large freshwater crustaceans and provide one of the richest sources of food for fast trout growth. To catch the very largest trout, bait fishermen usually prefer a softshell crayfish over any other live bait, even live sculpins. I've found that, in the same water, crayfish flies almost always catch larger trout than most other flies.

Crayfish have five pairs of legs on their thoracic segments. The first pair is enlarged and has strong, sharp jaws with pointed tips. They use these "pincers" or claws for capturing food, defense, and digging the burrows they live in. Crayfish eat most anything (plants, animals, and carrion) and are quite adept at catching live prey, such as small fish. Those same pincers will painfully pinch or cut you if you hold them carelessly. I've watched crayfish catch and eat trout parr in my aquariums by waving their antenna to attract the fish, then holding up and opening their brightly colored claw-tips to coax the trout to nip at them. Then with a quick snap, they close the pincer around the surprised little fish!

Crayfish vary in color from brown to olive to sandy gray, and most seem to adapt a color pattern and scheme that more or less mimics the environment they live in, however, I once

TOP AND SIDE VIEW OF CRAYFISH

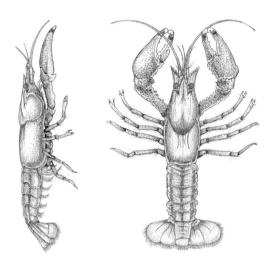

observed crayfish along the shorelines of Lake Superior that were blue and turquoise with bright, rusty red fringes on their appendages and tails! We have some beautiful gold and burnt umber species in many of our Ozark limestone streams.

Polly Rosborough, the great Oregon fly tier, once asked me to tie a dozen of my softshell crayfish for him. I was truly flattered, but also puzzled when he asked to make them with bright orange materials. I told him I thought only dead or cooked crayfish were orange. He said no, the live crayfish in Oregon, especially in his beloved Williamson River, almost glow in the dark they're so bright orange. Several years later, while fishing the Umpqua for steelhead, I saw big, gaudy orange crayfish crawling from rock to rock, just like Polly said! I'm still amazed that with that color they are not extinct.

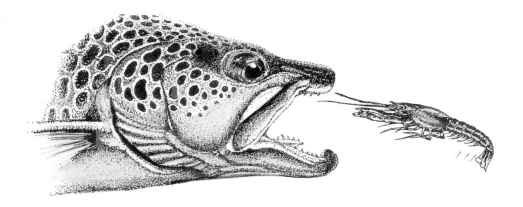

Crayfish, when threatened by trout, crawl or swim swiftly backwards to the nearest bottom crevice they can hide in.

Crayfish are widely distributed across North American trout streams, have a multi-annual life cycle, and are most active and can reproduce when water temps are above 45 degrees F. Below that, they are more or less dormant and stay deep down in their burrows until the water warms up in the spring. They forage and mate outside their burrows when water is warmer, growing rapidly. One to three times a season, crayfish shed their hard, armor-like exoskeleton skin to make space to grow into the larger skin that they secrete. During this skin exchange, they are very soft and more or less lethargic, which makes them the easiest prey for trout. They are called soft shells at this time and seem to have a more attractive odor in this vulnerable state because trout will move a long distance to catch and eat them. These soft crayfish are as easy for a trout to swallow whole as a piece of warm pasta.

Crayfish walk and forage forward on the bottom, but when they are threatened they raise their big defensive claws up, shuffle backwards or fold their legs, and swiftly swim with their strong abdominal segmented tail backwards to the nearest bottom structure crevice they can hide in. However, they are usually no match for a trout's speed and are easily captured. The tricky part for the trout that catches a hard-shelled crayfish is that it must first disable it while avoiding its claws and then swallow it tail first. Compared to a softshell, it's painful for a trout to eat hard shells live.

The best season to fish crayfish flies is late spring and all summer when they are most active and molting their skins. If you catch a trout that seems to have a full and lumpy belly, look down its mouth. Often, if it's crayfish being eaten, you'll see some antennae or claw tips protruding from the trout's throat. That's a good clue it's time to use crayfish flies.

Crayfish flies are most effective in low-light-level periods (a.m., p.m., and night) and when water levels are fluctuating. Trout prefer smaller sizes (12, 10, and 8) if they are hard shells and larger sizes (6, 4, and 10) when soft shells are available. Turn over rocks in the shallows to observe if crayfish are present, their state of molting, and their size and colors. A small aquarium net placed behind them is the best and safest way to capture them for closer observation.

I like to use a No. IV sink-tip line and three or four feet of leader to fish crayfish flies and cast them up and across stream riffles and shallow runs. A full-sinking line works better if you need to fish in a deep pool. A slow, erratic retrieve with the fly, right on the bottom, works the best. You need a lot of patience and focus to discern the difference between a strike and the constant feel of the fly bumping over bottom structures. But the reward for it is usually a big trout.

DAVE'S SOFTSHELL CRAYFISH

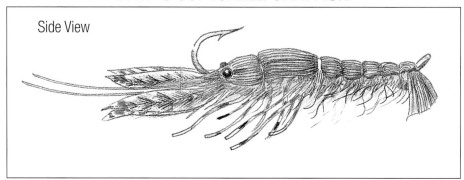

Side View

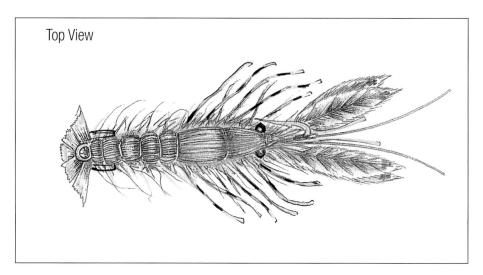

Top View

Crayfish imitation is tied backwards on an up-riding hook point and heavily weighted hook shank.

Crayfish flies should sink rapidly, be snag-proof, and should be shaped like a crayfish that's crawling or swimming backwards. They should be tied with materials that mimic the color and texture of the softshell. Softshells are usually lighter colored than hard shells or an orange-tan. There are dozens of crayfish flies commercially available and most of the imitations are tied with far too large pincers. They look good to you but look ominous to trout. Trout prefer less claw to tangle with and more meat to eat. Don't make the pincers more than one quarter of the total fly length. My best crayfish fly is the up-hook point Near Nuff Crayfish. I've caught nearly every species of fresh and many saltwater fish that eat crayfish, Pancora, and crabs with this fly.

This year, for better success, take a section of your fly box and stock it with crustaceans: scuds, sowbugs, and especially crayfish. When you suspect your water hides something much larger than you are catching, drift the bottom with a crayfish imitation.

More than likely you'll soon discover what awaits you there.

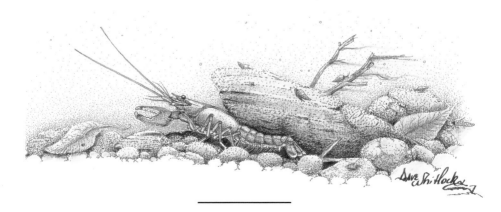

LEECHES

In the Annelid (worm) phylum, leeches are second only to earthworms in importance as food for trout. If trout loved pasta, earthworms would be their spaghetti and leeches their fettuccini. Experienced trout anglers appreciate leech imitations as an excellent way to tempt and catch larger trout, especially in still waters or back waters of streams.

Found mainly in cold-water ponds, lakes, marshes, and slow-flowing streams, there are approximately 44 species of leeches in North America. Among these there are several leech species that are terrestrial and marine. Leeches are typically called "bloodsuckers" by anglers and are envisioned by many moviegoers and swimmers as creepy water-vampires. Having had to remove several in my life, I'd tend to agree! Fortunately, most species feed on cold-blooded water-dwellers or scavenge on the dead. They rarely cause the death of their hosts. There are only a couple of leech species that attach to warm-blooded animals, and in medical history they were once extensively used on all manner of human infections and illnesses. In fact, they are enjoying somewhat of a

Trout forage for leeches on or near the bottoms of still waters or slow moving streams, especially those that are clear, rich in calcium carbonate, and have moderate to dense aquatic vegetation growth.

resurgence of popularity as the treatment of choice for limb attachment and venom removal.

The effect of a leech bite, other than its visual trauma, is minor, usually just some residual blood seepage due to an anticoagulant injected into the bite to keep the blood flowing. A shaving styptic pencil or flour and direct pressure will usually stop the bleeding. Wearing waders or wet-wading with long pants and socks virtually eliminates any chance of a leech run-in.

Most leeches I've sampled are attached to cold-blooded animals such as water turtles, live and dead fish, or fixed to the sides or bottom of a structure, resting. If you want to attract them, a fresh piece of meat seems to draw them quickest.

Leeches lack a rigid skeleton or exoskeleton. They are very muscular, dorsally flattened, and seem almost plastic. Narrow at the head and much thicker and wider at the posterior end, with a small oral sucker and a much larger caudal sucker, they can significantly lengthen themselves to swim or shorten and thicken themselves to feed, hide, or resist attacks. Each leech has 34 major true segments and numerous minor annuli (small folds on each segment) that are hard to see unless magnified. I doubt that even the most selective trout notice the segments, much less the annuli, when they see a tasty leech appear in their feeding lane.

The three orders of Hirudinea vary in color and markings. The literature I've read often speaks of how colorful they are, but the ones I've captured are usually camouflage shades of olive, brown, and dark gray with darker rows of spots, bars, or blotches with lighter tones on their undersides. I once sampled some 2.5- to 3.5-inch leeches in Lake of the Woods, Canada that were chocolate black on top and a rich burnt orange on their underside. If you look very closely, you can see five sets of tiny eyes in an arch around the top of their heads near their mouths. But again, I'm sure trout could care less how many eyeballs a leech has.

Leeches move on structures by looping with their two suckers sort of like inchworms. They also simply creep along the bottom, and some actively swim with a nose-to-tail, undulating up-and-down action. Because they breathe through their skin by osmosis, they don't require as high a level of dissolved oxygen as many aquatic insects and fish. But they do not thrive well in acid or murky water. In fact, the higher the concentration of alkaline or lime, the better for most species. Those calcium-carbonate rich, spring-fed streams, or ponds lush with aquatic vegetation are ideal for leech life.

LEECH SHAPES

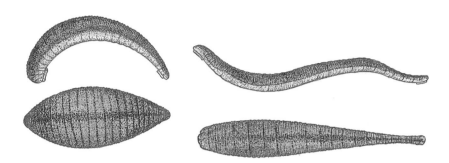

Having no skeleton but being very muscular, leeches can change their shape to accommodate their needs. At left shows the top and side view of the leech shape while resting, hiding, or feeding. At right is the leech shape while swimming.

CHAMOIS LEECH FLY

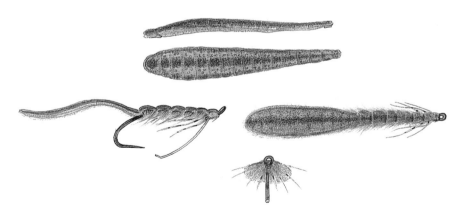

The swimming leech is easily imitated with a strip of chamois leather shaped, sized, and colored like the original. A snag guard and open-loop knot complete the effectiveness.

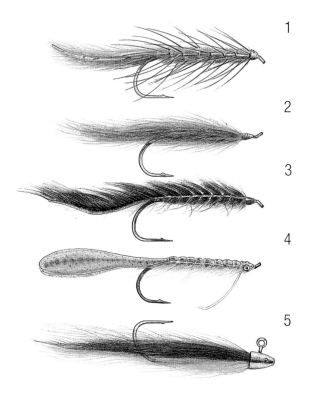

Five Popular Leech Flies

1. Woolly Bugger
2. Marabou Leech
3. Rabbit Hair Strip Fly
4. Whitlock's Chamois Leech
5. Marabou Jig

Reproduction occurs by hermaphroditic coupling with another bisexual leech (all leeches are that way). Eggs are then extruded in small cocoons. Most leeches live between two to ten years if not eaten before then. Many don't survive for long, though, because they are relished by most species of fish, birds, crayfish, and turtles. But, for some reason, I seldom see them on menus at fine French or Italian restaurants.

LEECHES

Leeches are easy to imitate and simple to fish properly. Lure fisherman use very realistic, molded, plastic leeches that are often even scented. For fly fishing, patterns like wooly buggers, marabou leeches, chamois leeches, wooly worms, mini-marabou jigs, and mohair leeches are great simulators. Because these creatures swim slowly and usually stay close to the bottom of the water column, the trick to good leeching for trout is to work the fly *deep* and *very slowly.* Marabou, chamois leathers, and ostrich herl make the best tails for leeches because each move so realistically in water. My chamois leech design is probably the most realistically shaped, textured, and moving imitation I've ever designed.

Leeching in still waters is the most popular and my favorite method is to use a slow-sinking, snag-proof leech fly that I can swim with a slow, up-and-down action, fished on a clear, slow-sinking (intermediate) fly line. I use a short (four- to six-foot) knotless leader and a fluorocarbon tippet. I drop my rod tip close to the water and count the fly down to get it deep and then begin a slow, erratic retrieve—and I hold on! Strikes can be sudden and vicious and you need to be prepared to set the hook slowly and softly in order to avoid instant break-offs. I often use an open Duncan loop knot to help absorb the trout's strike shock.

In streams, a dead-drifted leech fly works especially well. The real magic to leeching in flowing water happens by using a strike indicator set to suspend the leech fly or marabou jig just above the bottom. The surface chop in a riffle or wind chop wavelets will animate the indicator which likewise seductively animates the leech fly with the perfect amount of subtle action to attract big, hungry trout to your leech as it progresses, at the speed of the current, downstream.

Leeches are predominately nocturnal and so imitations naturally work best on very low-light days: at dawn, dusk, or at night. I've found that all black leech flies, with only one or two strands of pearl or silver crystal flash or flashabou, to be very effective. Fishing a leech fly slow and low at night through structure is much more practical if the hook point swims up or if it has a nylon, monofilament snag guard.

Leeches, like earthworms, are not the classic, delicate foods we often prefer to imitate to catch trout. But, however ugly they might be, they truly are a delicious, cinch-to-catch sight to big trout. For that matter, they are also irresistible to carp, smallmouth bass, sunfish, largemouth bass, catfish, walleye, and the like. Just try it.

Earthworms: Terrestrial and Aquatic

U nder certain circumstances, three pseudo-flies—earthworms, fish eggs, and fish pellets—can be as effective for trout as imitations of traditional trout foods. For years, I had rigid prejudices against using flies that imitate these "bait-like" food forms. But with maturity, I've gained a much more open mind and have come to accept them when circumstances are present that make traditional flies truly inappropriate or inadequate. I'll address earthworms in this chapter.

Earthworms

One person's trash is often another's treasure, and that's especially so when it comes to catching trout that aren't feeding on a hatch, crustaceans, or minnows. Terrestrial and aquatic earthworms are one of the truly perfect live, natural baits for trout and nearly every other species of predator, omnivore, and scavenger fish living in still and flowing

Aquatic and terrestrial earthworms are most often available to trout during excessive water rises caused by rain runoff or tailwater fluctuations. Imitations should have colors that are visible in murky waters and should be drifted just off the bottom.

freshwaters in North America. They are widely distributed, plentiful, easy to catch, and very rich in food value. Trout seem to truly love them. In my teens and twenties, I loved to bait fish with four-pound ultra light spin tackle and my favorite baits were a can of earthworms and a bucket of softshell crayfish. Only a gill net or dynamite could be more productive in catching trout. Finally, when I was converted by Lee Wulff to catch-and-release, I stopped using these live baits. At the same time, as converts sometimes do, I developed a definite negative attitude toward bait fishing or using flies that imitate bait.

Terrestrial and aquatic earthworms are very physically similar and only recently were classed separately. The main difference of interest for anglers is that terrestrial earthworms dwell in the earth along stream and lake banks and aquatic earthworms dwell mainly in the soil below the water line. Both have similar feeding, reproduction, and life cycles. The specifics of these activities are of far less concern to the trout fisherman than aquatic insects are, for successful timing and imitation. The most important thing to understand is that earthworms are most often available to trout when high water or sudden fluctuations are occurring. At that time, worms can be washed from their soil burrows. Often, especially at night or after a heavy rain, earthworms are active and near the soil surface and are very likely to be washed into drainages of streams or swept off shorelines into ponds and lakes. Trout will take immediate advantage of this rich feeding opportunity.

Because of constant water fluctuations, many cold tailwater rivers provide trout with lots of earthworms that are dislodged from banks and bottom sediments. I've had excellent results using worm imitations on the White River below the Bullshoals Dam in Arkansas when sudden large volumes of hydro-generation water flush the bottom and make the water roily and opaque with sediment. This is one of those occasions when it's difficult to catch trout on dries, wetflies, or nymphs, but when

AQUATIC EARTHWORM

the worm works its very best. So, you'll find that imitations of these tasty, strongly odored, one- to five-inch sections of trout spaghetti are usually most effective after a heavy rain or snow melt, or right after hydro-electric generation begins. Fishing in very cold water to lethargic trout is another situation where a worm imitation works, especially if you fish it close to the bottom in slow, deep runs or at tops of pools.

Since worms do not swim or emerge to hatch, simply fish them tumbled along close to the bottom with the speed and direction of the current. Usually a floating line, long leader, and tippet with an indicator and split shot accomplishes this most efficiently. Experimenting with lengths and colors is also often necessary because trout might be selective to naturals or because the lower visibility water conditions may require larger or more highly visible colors. Most likely, too, they might be simply highly visible attractors to trout. Red is the most popular with fly fishers, however brown, orange, pink, tan, purple, and chartreuse are other colors that often out-fish each other. Live terrestrial earthworms are usually a rich, almost iridescent reddish brown.

The four main groups of terrestrial earthworms are night crawlers, field worms, manure worms, and red worms. When I was a kid, we called all fishing worms "red worms" because of the coloration. The true aquatic worms that I've collected while sampling streams for trout foods are a vivid dark pink or scarlet red and are from one to two inches in length. It's not uncommon in organically rich, silt-laden waters to find more worms than any other natural food. The most popular worm fly design is, of course, the San Juan worm, and it is probably most responsible for the current popularity of imitating aquatic worms. Having such a simple

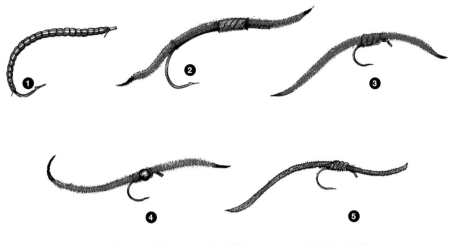

AQUATIC EARTHWORM IMITATIONS

*1. Red vinyl ribbed worm on large English style bait hook
*2. Ultra-chenille worm tied on English style bait hook
 3. Ultra-chenille worm tied on small, short-shank hook
 4. Tungsten bead chenille worm
 5. Suede leather worm

*No longer popular for catch-and-release fly fishers because of the large size of their hooks, which can increase trout mortality.

form of no legs, wings, tails, or antenna, most worm flies are constructed with just a piece of nylon ultra-chenille on small, short shank hooks. The ends of the chenille are shaped to a natural taper by heating them with a small flame from a lighter or candle. The first San Juan worm flies I saw were constructed on curved shank, size eight, six, or four

English bait or caddis hooks and clear red vinyl jibbing material. These looked very wormy and were extremely effective but as deadly to trout as swallowed live bait on barbed hooks. Trout took them greedily and deep into their gill-throat areas and so they were nearly always lethally hooked. Another bad effect of the large English bait hook was that it often blinded one eye of the fish because the bend and gape was so large it passed up through the roof of a trout's mouth and into one of its eyes.

SNAG-PROOF WORM IMITATIONS

Because earthworm imitations are most effective drifted near or on the bottom, they often encounter obstructions.

1. A worm imitation without a snag guard often ends up lost.
2a. & 2b. Worm imitations with a simple nylon monofilament guard seldom hang up, thus can be fished more effectively.

Most catch-and-release fly fishers, guides, and fly shops stopped using them and some catch-and-release areas even outlawed them.

Today, most worm flies, despite their lengths (one to four inches), are tied on size 12, 14, and 16 short-shank barbless hooks which usually only lip or jaw hook. A tungsten bead on the hook is probably a better weighting option than tungsten or lead split-shot on the tippet because it will sink the fly quickly, hang up less frequently, and tangle the leader far less. When fishing around lots of tree roots, aquatic vegetation, or rocky crevices, you'll probably hang up and lose a lot of worm flies unless you tie or buy them with a nylon monofilament snag guard. This simple monofilament loop on a worm fly will allow it to be confidently fished deeply and over bottom structures without so many hang-ups . . .and with many more strikes!

By carrying one or two dozen assorted colors and lengths in your nymph box, you have the perfect insurance fly when trout get hard to raise due to murky, high, cold, or fluctuating waters that limit trout's interest or choice of foods. If nothing seems to work, try an earthworm fly, and when someone asks you why you are doing so well, tell them you are "free-swimming an aquatic annelid." Sounds so much better than "fishin' a worm" . . . and they're bound to be impressed.

FIVE

Terrestrials

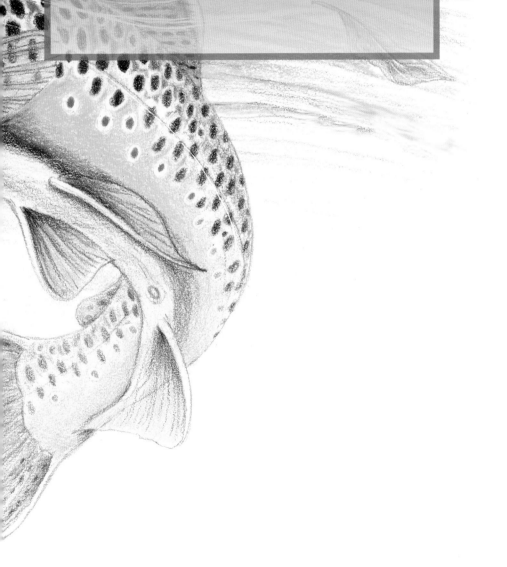

Terrestrial Insects—

Ants and Beetles

T errestrial insects are a major group of insects that trout depend upon for food, and close, dense, streamside vegetation contributes greatly to increased populations of this important category of insects. I got to thinking about how very much I enjoy fishing with terrestrials and decided to feature this group in the book, and to share my enthusiasm with you. Terrestrial insects are land-born, air-breathing insects that vastly outnumber aquatic insects in species and quantity. Few are designed to float or swim, so, if they're not there to drink, contact with trout streams and still waters usually means sinking and drowning or becoming an instant meal. I'd say that most terrestrial insects that are eaten by trout are victims of their own crawling or flying mistakes or of environmental conditions such as high winds, cold snaps, or floods. Often, too, when certain winged terrestrials living near water swarm to mate, many end up falling in.

Young larvae or nymphs of terrestrial insects seldom reach trout waters, so unlike similar stages of aquatic insects, they are not important forms for fly fishers. This certainly simplifies terrestrial fishing for us, because we just need to recognize and imitate the size and color of the adult stage.

The latitudes that usually provide water temperatures cold enough annually to hold resident trout have cold weather during late fall, winter, and early spring. The terrestrial insects in these areas are most abundant and active enough to end up in a trout stream from summer to late fall. In general, I'd say the prime time for catching trout on terrestrial imitations is July, August, September, and October. This is nice timing because many major aquatic insect hatches have ended and trout are switching to terrestrials, extending our dry fly and surface fishing throughout the late summer and fall.

Trout that are feeding on aquatic hatches can get very selective about what particular insect, size, and color they will take, as there are often huge numbers of the same insect on the water at the same time. About the time most aquatic insect hatches finish for the year, (approximately mid-summer), adult terrestrials start showing up in appreciable numbers. At that point, trout must become opportunists, because their food choices are never the same day to day, and they only see one to a few of the same insects on the water at the same time. Occasionally, a large swarm of flying ants or a small plague of beetles may suddenly blow down onto a stream or lake surface, triggering a selective, trout-feeding frenzy. But on most days during the warmer months, trout spend much more time "looking up" and listening for that characteristic *plop* of a terrestrial gone astray.

Although terrestrials do sink, most float momentarily, so the majority of terrestrial imitations are dry or surface flies, and for me, that's the most fun. However, fishing them wet can also be *very* effective. Whichever method you choose, remember to focus at all times on your fly because you never know what kind of strike to expect. Sometimes a trout will streak out from under a bank and slam-dunk your fly with a swirl and a splash, while your very next cast might bring the most subtle of sippers. Of course, that's all part of the magic.

There are countless species of terrestrial insects, but trout fly fishers only need to imitate about a dozen. I suggest having a separate terrestrial fly box that you put in your vest from mid-summer to later fall. Fill it with imitations of ants, beetles, grasshoppers, crickets, cicadas, leafhoppers, bees, hornets, leaf worms, moths, and spiders. In this chapter, we'll discuss ants and beetles.

Ants and Beetles

Ants (order Hymenoptera) and beetles (order Coleoptera) are the two most common and annually abundant terrestrials available to trout. They have clearly distinctive silhouettes that most trout seem to readily recognize and to which they willingly rise. I've actually seen trout ignore aquatic insects hatching and instead go for ants or beetles falling on the water's surface. A small black ant or beetle pattern (size 16, 14, or 12) will often immediately raise a big trout that has ignored my best match-the-hatch presentations.

Concentrate on fishing ants and beetles along the perimeter of a stream where there are abundant overhanging tree limbs or plants and grasses. Look for occasional, slow, deliberate, subtle rises at times when

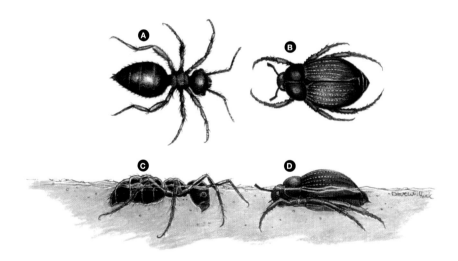

A. Ant—top view
B. Beetle—top view
C. Ant—side view in water. (Note low float profile.)
D. Beetle—side view in water. (Note low float profile.)

no adult aquatic insects are active. Most likely this will be trout eating ants or beetles. Fish these imitations as precisely as possible, and aim for drag-free-drift. This summer and fall terrestrial fishing usually means low, slow, and clear stream conditions and, in turn, spookier trout. Be as stealthy as possible with your dress, approach, and presentations. Fly tackle for ants and beetles should be on the light side, with 1 to 4 weight rods and lines and long, light leaders and tippet.

Because of their small, dark profiles that ride low in the surface film, these ant and beetle flies can be nearly impossible to track visually, especially for "over-40" eyes. "When I was young, I never liked fishing ants and beetles until I got the idea of putting a fluorescent tuft of yarn on the back of each fly. This "bright spot" definitely improved my sighting, drifting, and hook-setting ability. It's also been my experience that these colored spots attract more strikes to the fly . . . maybe they help the trout

BEETLE AND ANT IMITATIONS WITH BRIGHT SPOT BACKS

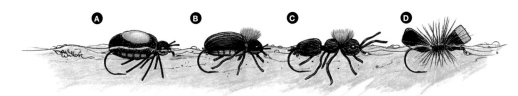

A. Foam beetle with painted bright spot back
B. Deer Hair Japanese beetle with yarn bright spot
C. Dave's Deer Hair Carpenter Ant with yarn bright spot
D. McMurray Foam Ant with bright-spot head

Trout seem to like the taste and easy capture of ants and beetles and will often take an ant or beetle during a stretch when they refuse to take the best match-the-hatch flies.

see them too! I highly recommend you tie or buy terrestrials with these bright spots.

Today, most ant and beetle imitations are tied with close-cell foam, dubbing, or deer hair bodies and rubber or deer hair legs. The best ant colors are black or rusty brown; black, brown, or green are the three best beetle colors. Some beetles have definite iridescent blue or green sheens that you might want to imitate.

These days I really look forward to the terrestrial season. I often will take days or parts of days and just meticulously search the water close to the shoreline and around the perimeter of structures with ant or beetle imitations. This has added another pleasurable dimension to my surface trout fishing, with the extra bonus of often catching larger trout than I usually do on aquatic insect imitations during that time of the summer.

Enjoy!

GRASSHOPPERS AND CRICKETS

In a trout's world, the most important terrestrial insects are probably ants and beetles because of their universal abundance and long season of availability. But in a trout *fly fisher's* world, I rate hoppers and crickets over ants and beetles for moving the most mature and largest trout to rise to the surface for one juicy bite. It has been my experience that once a trout feeds on either of these Orthoptera, they get very excited and boldly aggressive whenever a hopper or cricket plops on the surface near them. They even seem to lose that natural caution that allowed them to get so big in the first place. It's as though these insects contain some very addictive hopper narcotic!

Short-horned Grasshoppers (Acrididae)

Short-horned grasshoppers are the most common hopper found near water and begin their life cycle as eggs laid in the late summer or

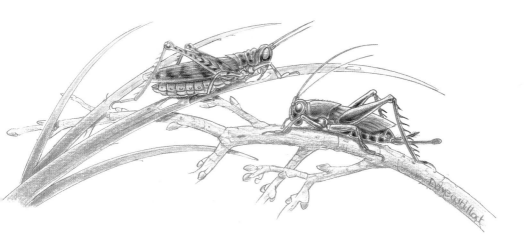

fall or occasionally in mid-spring. After hatching, the little tan or olive nymphs are flightless and live concealed in weeds and grass, much like mayfly and stonefly nymphs live along the rocky, weedy bottom of a stream. Maturing in size, color, and mobility by mid-summer, these now-adult hoppers become much more visible and audible as they hop, click, and fly about, seeking mates or greener pastures on which to feed. The lush, tender streambank grasses, irrigated by the flowing water, attract summer-hungry hoppers like iron filings to a magnet. Adult hopper season usually extends into September and October, depending on the weather, and even into November in midwestern and southwestern states.

To my knowledge, grasshoppers do not go to water to drink but, rather, are apt to take an unplanned crash landing and swim while they are mating or flying (especially on windy days), during sudden thunderstorms, or when flushed by animals or machines used for pasture harvesting. Many seem to have no sense about avoiding water as they splash down.

The best times to hopper-fish each day are usually from around 11 AM until 5 to 6 PM, when the weather is warm and windy. Hoppers and crickets usually make a noisy, splashy *plop* as they crash-land into the water just off the bank, which is pure music to nearby trout ears. Since they are not designed to float on the surface like adult aquatic insects, they have to struggle just to stay afloat long enough to reach the dry safety of the stream or lake shoreline. Most will kick in the direction of the shoreline from which they flew. In fact, if the surface of a stream or lake is choppy, hoppers will often drown eventually. A deadly way to catch trout is to use a hopper fly and add a split shot 10 or 12 inches up the leader from the fly or use a weighted hopper.

My first trout hopper catches in 1952 (when I was seventeen) were with a fly rod baited with lively, kicking and squirming grasshoppers and a split shot. Dan Bailey, during my first visit to his Livingston, Montana

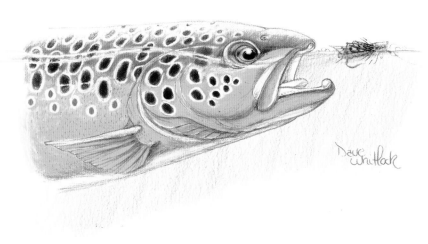

From July through November, selective, mature trout will rise aggressively to the *plop* of a grasshopper on the surface.

DAVE'S CRICKET

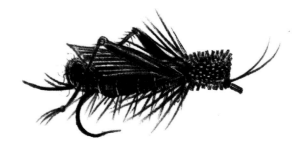

WHIT HOPPER

A. Bright spot for tracking and strike detection

B. Weed guard for bank grasses or woody structures

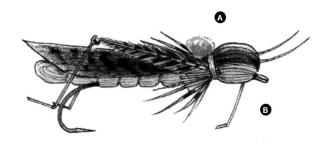

shop, told me I could do almost as well with a Joe's Hopper fly . . . and boy was he right! That advice changed a lot of my fly-fishing fortunes! Just like the monster trout that rose to my hopper flies, I became "hooked" on *hoppertunity* for a lifetime!

Crickets (Gryllidae)

Crickets are the vocal, nocturnal counterparts of grasshoppers. Their life cycle, feeding, and growth mostly parallel those of grasshoppers. Although there are quite a number of distinctive species of crickets, bush, field and ground crickets are the sub-families most often available to fish. These terrestrials are approximately ½" to 1¾" in length, are shaped similarly and are usually colored black, dark brown, or tan. Tan ground crickets are raised by the millions commercially as live food for pets and fishing bait. In the summer and fall, cricket flies will attract trout to the surface in the daytime, but they are even more effective for those who fly fish for big trout at night. I remember reading a story around 30 to 40 years ago, written about a famous Pennsylvania spring creek terrestrial fly fisher who located a monstrous night-feeding brown trout in a stream that ran through the downtown section of a small city. After a great deal of effort and a large assortment of flies, he eventually caught it on a Letort cricket. I was so impressed, I tied an entire boxful of crickets!

SURFACE FLOAT PROFILES OF HOPPER FLIES AND LIVE GRASSHOPPERS

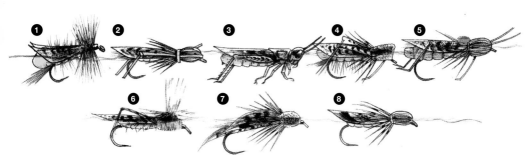

1. Joe's Hopper
2. Lawson's Hopper
3. Grasshopper
4. Dave's Hopper
5. Whit Hopper
6. Schroeder's Parachute Hopper
7. Muddler Minnow
8. Gartside Pheasant Hopper

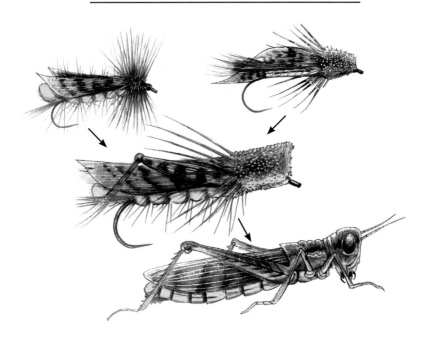

I incorporated the best physical features, materials, and colors of Joe's Hopper, the Muddler Minnow, and large kicklegs to tie my popular Dave's Hopper, a fly few big trout can resist.

A key to triggering those big, terrestrial-loving trout is to present your hopper and cricket flies with a definite, splashy, *plop* sound. That's what live ones do when they hit the water.

Thus, imitations should be tied densely and float low in the surface film to be most effective. Casting and fishing close to grassy, undercut stream banks, sheer higher-cut banks, and fallen trees lying close and parallel to stream banks is very effective; the best of these prime areas are those with consistent, prevailing offshore winds. I'd recommend using a bug-taper fly line and bass leader to make these presentations in such windy situations.

Hopper and cricket flies also perform better if they have snag guards so they can be safely cast very close to grassy banks, under willows, next to fallen tree roots, trunks, and limbs. Night-fished crickets definitely require snag guards because it's harder to judge presentation accuracy in the dark.

Try a natural drift with some kick and swim animation. However, it's been my experience that often a big hopper lover will blast the hopper fly so quickly there is no time to animate. Just remember, when a trout makes a showy, bass-like attack on your fly, don't strike too quickly or too hard . . . give him a second, and then take your time to set the hook smoothly. Because they love hoppers so much, trout seldom eject the fly quickly.

Fly shops offer lots of hopper choices these days. Usually sizes 12, 10, and 8 are best for most situations. Those that have a low float profile, distinctive kicker legs, and either yellow, tan, or olive undersides are what most trout seem to be looking for. Be sure the barb is pinched down, as trout tend to take hopper and cricket flies aggressively and deeply.

One final suggestion: From spring to early winter, if you are not sure what surface fly to use, instead of a Royal Wulff or a Stimulator, try a size 10 or 8 yellow-bellied Dave's Hopper or Black Cricket. It often seems they can attract big trout at the least expected time and place. Maybe it's because big trout never forget just how good their last hopper dinner tasted!

Moths and Caterpillars

Moths and their caterpillars are in the family of Lepidoptera, which also includes butterflies. This is a large group of terrestrial insects that provides trout with abundant meal opportunities throughout the spring, summer and fall months. Varying greatly in size, number, and color patterns, the numerous smaller, more somber-colored ones are the most important for fly fishers to imitate.

Moths and caterpillars can also provide the terrestrial fly fisher with lots of special surface-fly action. Over the years, many of my most memorable encounters with these critters have happened unexpectedly. That's because, like ants and beetles, we usually don't study specific species of moths and caterpillars enough to know when and where to intercept them in significant numbers when they are on or near trout waters.

For instance, one July morning about twenty years ago, I was in Montana fishing lovely Rock Creek with Frank Johnson. Frank told me the evening before that we would need to be on the water by 8:00 AM to hit the *spruce moths flight to* drink. I'd never heard of such a thing,

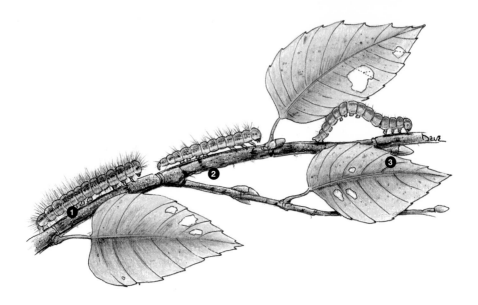

Caterpillars feasting on leaves of trees and shrubs that overhang trout streams often fall off, extending a tiny web that holds them above or on the water, making them a sitting duck for big, feeding trout.

There are three general body forms of caterpillars:
1. very fuzzy
2. moderately fuzzy
3. naked

Trout and most other fish prefer 2 and 3.

but sure enough, between 9:00 AM and noon that day, a blizzard of big, tan moths began flying from the spruce trees straight down to the water to drink. The instant reaction this triggered was incredible—big brown, rainbow, and cutthroat began rising everywhere! Using size 10 and 12 elk-hair caddis, I soon lost track of how many big trout we hooked.

I remember another time, late one June on the Pere Marquette River in Michigan, when I was surprised to see a big brown, right at midday, rising noisily under low, overhanging alders and willows. I could not figure out what he was so excited about until my eyes caught a glimpse of a series of silvery webs, glinting in the sunlight. At the lower edge of the webs were inch-long, bright green little caterpillars . . . some dangling a foot or so above the water and others floating on the water's surface making small V-wakes. I searched my terrestrial fly box for my green, deer-hair inchworm fly. I found it and tied it on. Soon that big brown rose to my fly and took it. I couldn't believe it! Unfortunately, he also immediately dove under a log and broke my 4x tippet. Later, a Pere Marquette guide told me that in those situations I could cast through the webs, dropping many more "worms" onto the water and chumming up many more big trout.

Moths, like caddis, have a complete-phase life cycle: egg, larva, pupa, and adult. The caterpillar is the larval stage, after which most caterpillars form some sort of pupal cocoon on the branches or leaves of bushes and trees on which they feed. Very simplified, caterpillars have three general body types: 1) very fuzzy, 2) moderately fuzzy, 3) naked. Fish mainly prefer the semi-fuzzy and naked ones. In fact, some fuzzy species have an unpleasant toxin that some birds and fish dislike. I've seen bass, trout, and sunfish in my pond refuse fuzzy tent caterpillars while the catfish gobbled them down.

To my knowledge, there's not much point in trying to imitate moth pupae because they seldom come in contact with trout waters. (If anyone reading this knows of trout feeding on moth pupae, I'd like to hear the details.)

Moths are mostly nocturnal so they are especially plentiful to trout at night, and fish will often feed on them all night long. Trout ponds and streams with dock or street lights attract *hordes* of moths from spring until the fall nights get too chilly.

Imitating Caterpillars

I don't recommend using caterpillar flies unless you see large numbers of them in the bushes and branches that overhang the water. However, if they are present, it is a good bet that the mid-day rises you see or hear will be to these caterpillars, and by all means try to capture a sample and imitate it. Fish them dapped on the surface as if they were still attached to their webs from an upstream position or plopped down and dead-drifted from up, across, or downstream. I tie mine mostly out of buoyant materials like deer hair, elk rump hair, or Rainy's foam rubber cylinders. I put a snag guard on each fly so I can drift it right under overhanging trees and close to shrub limbs. Also, a bright spot on its back helps to see and track the drift. Yellow, bright green, and dirty olive seem to be the best colors.

CATERPILLAR IMITATIONS

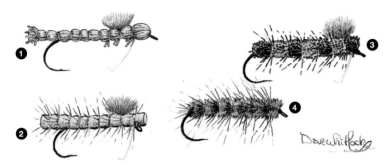

1. Whitlock's Green Inchworm with bright spot and snag guard
2. Rainy's foam cylinder caterpillar with bright spot and snag guard
3. Clipped deer-hair caterpillar with bright spot and snag guard
4. Wet chenille caterpillar
   Flies 1, 2, and 3 float in surface film and 4 is subsurface.

MOTH IMITATIONS

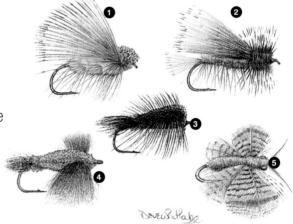

1. Elk-hair caddis, but tied with bulkier wings and body to imitate the moth's thicker shape
2. Kauffman's Stimulator—tan
3. Whitlock Hair Gerbubble Night Moth—black or white are best night colors
4. Whitlock's Marabou Winged Deer-hair Moth
5. Partridge Spent-Wing Moth

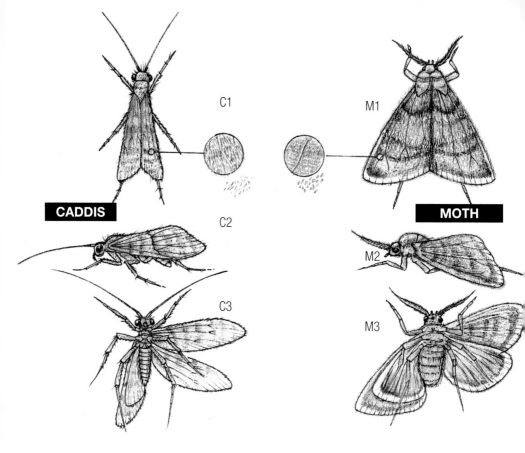

Moths and adult caddis flies can be the same general size and appear very similar. To identify each:

CADDIS (LEFT)

Cl. Top view.

   Antennae are long and thin.

   Folded wings have a narrow, tent-like outline.

   Wings are hairy.

C2. Side view

C3. Underside view

   Body detail with one pair of wings folded and one pair extended.

MOTH (RIGHT)

M1. Top view

   Antennae are fuzzy and fern-shaped.

142

      Folded wings are wide and delta-shaped.

      Wings are scaly.

M2.   Side view

M3.   Underside view

      Body detail with one pair of wings folded and one pair extended. (Note that the moth body is much larger and fuzzier.)

Imitating Moths

The most practical moths to imitate are those active and numerous smaller ones, sizes 6 to 14. These resemble caddis adults in flight, but at rest their wings are more delta-shaped, where the caddis wings are more tent-shaped. Moth wings are covered with tiny scales that come off easily if held, while caddis wings are hairy and don't seem to shed off easily to touch. Their bodies are fatter than caddis adults, antennae usually shorter and fuzzier, and legs shorter. If you had to select one color pattern, I'd say a light tan body and light brown wings. Fish your moth imitations with variable action from twitching and skittering to dead drifts. This is most easily done from an upstream position, casting across and downstream, day or nighttime.

Moths are best imitated by using such flared-hair-wing-dry flies as Troth's Elk Hair Caddis and Kaufman's Stimulators in the size and general color of the moths you see flying about or landing on the water. You can also use spent-wing caddis designs tied with partridge, sharp-tail grouse, or hen-pheasant body feathers to imitate their four large, intricately marked opaque wings.

One summer, between my first and second year of college, I got a job at a fishing lodge guiding in Ontario, Canada near Kenora. That

June and July there was a horde of fuzzy caterpillars that the locals called "armyworms" stripping most of the birch trees of their leaves. They even made the paved highways slick as they were crushed crawling across while searching for more food. When these caterpillars pupated, they produced millions of fat-bodied, size 6, brown moths. Kenora was almost shut down at night for several weeks as millions of moths were attracted to the city lights. But the good news was that every trout, whitefish, bass, walleye, and yellow perch fed all day and all night on the floating rafts of moths. A simple, small, size 6 or 4, brown, spent-moth, deerhair bug caught big fish for us until our arms gave out.

Keep your eyes and ears on alert between May and November for caterpillars and moths. They can produce some very unique and spectacular terrestrial surface fly fishing.

CICADAS

icadas are one cool bug, and from time to time (like grasshoppers and crickets) can offer the opportunistic terrestrial fly fisher superb buggin' trout encounters from late spring to late fall. A certain fast-food chain advertises to "think outside the bun." I say "think outside of ants, beetles, and hoppers," and carry a few cicada flies to jazz up your summer fly fishing on still or flowing trout and bass waters.

Cicadas are large, bulky, periodic, and very vocal terrestrial insects which are usually heard before they're seen when you are near woodlands. The sound usually brings back late-summertime childhood memories. They produce an undulating, raspy song and are numerous and quite common in many parts of the world. Of the approximately 75 species in North America, 5 or 6 are significant for fly fishers. They are a major trout food in New Zealand.

Cicadas have a relatively simple life cycle of egg, nymph, and adult. The eggs are deposited on the ends of certain deciduous tree branches. After hatching, the nymph spends a few weeks feeding on the branch tip, causing the end of the branch to die and eventually fall from the tree. Moving to the ground, the nymph burrows down to the tree-root system, feeding on tree sap and remaining there for 3 to 17 years, depending on the particular cicada species. When conditions and timing are right, huge numbers of the same species will dig back out from underground, crawl up the tree trunk, split their skin dorsally, and emerge as adults. For a couple of weeks to a month or more they sing almost constantly and mate. Many of these adults eventually fall prey to wasps, hornets, birds, squirrels, and frogs. It's only adults that are active in trees near or over water that are of interest and benefit to trout and other insect-eating fish. Most species of adult cicada are a real mouthful, running from 18 to 40 mm. Mature trout seem to know them well and enthusiastically gorge on as many as they possibly can as often as they are available.

The most spectacular cicada is the 17-year "locust," *magicicadas septendecin.*

This relatively small, red-eyed, blackbodied, orange-legged species emerges in astronomical numbers every 13 to 17 years; incredible hordes of adults usually show up in May or early June, checker-boarded across large areas, with groups of the 17-year hatches emerging in different areas every year or so. Some states' agricultural departments have emergence maps available. Those I have witnessed in Oklahoma, Arkansas, and Missouri literally pave the water surface, and every trout, bass sunfish, catfish, carp, sucker, chub, and walleye will rise and hog them down until they nearly explode. I'd hate to encounter such an opportunity without some flies to imitate them.

Besides the 13- to 17-year species, other species emerge more frequently from May to September but in far fewer numbers. Most are green, black, and brown, and have clear, coarsely veined, cellophane-like wings. The big green and black "dog days" cicadas that I remember hearing and catching as a child emerge every three to five years, and there are always some hatching midsummer throughout the Southeast and Northeast.

CICADAS

A. Cicada nymph. Nymphs are not available to trout.
B. Top view of midsummer adult cicada
C. Side view of same
D. Top view of spent-wing, 17-year periodic cicada

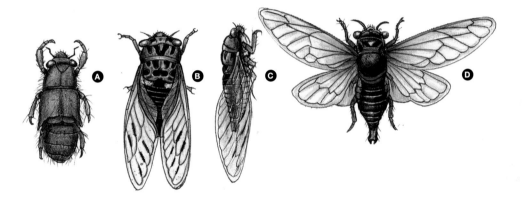

Some of my most vivid memories of cicada fishing have been on Utah's Flaming Gorge tailwater section of the Green River, on Missouri and Arkansas Ozark streams, and on the incredible trout rivers of both islands of New Zealand. It always seems that the largest fish in the area greedily rise to the splashy plop of a size 8, 6, or 4 cicada pattern.

Nothing, except perhaps hoppers, brings big mature trout to the surface of difficult, clear, low-water conditions better than a cicada fly. Adult cicada imitations, like large adult stonefly and hopper flies, allow the fly fisher to raise, hook, and successfully land the largest of 5-pound-plus trout because you can present them nicely on 6- and 7-weight fly

Cicadas are large, opportunistic terrestrials that excite big trout to the surface with splashy entry and fluttering, spent wings.

tackle and shorter, stronger leaders. I recommend no less than 3x tippets for cicada imitations.

Imitations should be presented near or beneath overhanging tree limbs with an audible *plop* and animated as if they were fluttering to swim and escape the water surface. I prefer spent-wing imitations tied with snag guards so they can be cast very close to tree limbs. Though some trout rush them on impact, others will hesitate, drop back, and then turn and smash the fly. I once watched a really big New Zealand brown take two looks at a size 8 black cicada fly, refuse, swim away, and then turn back and rush 6 or 8 feet downstream to inhale the fly in a frightening splash. Then, for a grand finale, the impulsive cicada-eater bit the tippet and released me from my fly.

Cicada bodies can be made of deer hair, molded sponge rubber, or sponge rubber–sheet wafer sandwiches. Their wings can be well-imitated with pearl crystal flash, hackle or buck tail and most are tied with six or eight rubber legs. I'd advise adding a clear monofilament snag guard as well. There are several commercial cicada flies available. Even bass poppers, hairbugs, chunky hoppers, and adult stoneflies in the correct color and size can work well for cicada imitation.

Keep your ears and eyes on alert from spring to fall, ask about them while in local tackle shops, check website reports and inspect the waters for the emergences of cicadas. They are a sheer joy for the opportunistic, cold- and warm-water fly fisher to hear and experience.

HOW TO ATTACH A SNAG GUARD

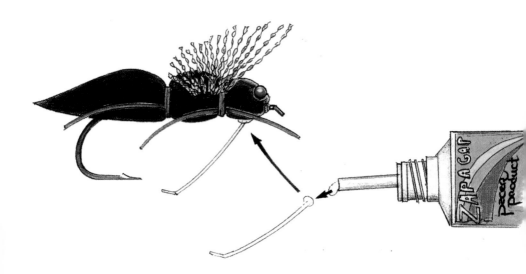

To fish cicada imitations most effectively, they should be presented close to the overhanging tree limbs from which the naturals fall. Most commercial imitations do not have snag guards, but it's easy to put one on. Here's how:

A. Cut a filament of hard mason nylon mono, approximately ⅔ the diameter of the hook wire, to a length just slightly longer than the hook gape. Bend a ⅛-inch foot on the end.

B. Place a small drop of Zap-A-Gap or five-minute epoxy on the other end of the nylon mono strand.

C. Push mono end with Zap into the fly head as shown and hold until cement sets. Some materials like balsa, foam rubber, or closed-cell plastic foam may need a small hole punched or drilled into the head before mono and cement can be inserted.

POPULAR ADULT CICADA FLY DESIGNS

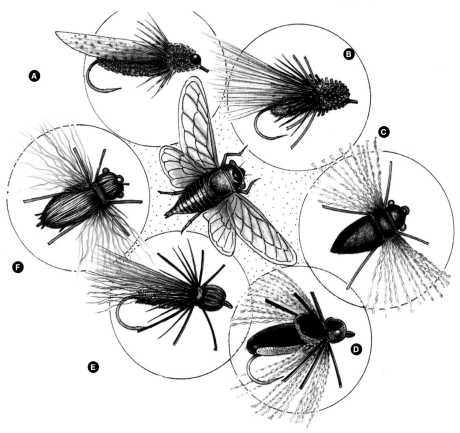

A. Reids Cicada
B. Deer Hair Cicada
C. Whitlock's Spent-Wing Cicada
D. Steeves Disc Head Cicada
E. Stalcup's Cicada
F. Elk-Hair Cicada

Jassids, or Leaf and Tree Hoppers

I'd like to introduce or re-introduce you to some important smaller members of Homoptera, the tiny, super abundant, widely distributed leaf and tree hoppers. I've titled this chapter "jassids," borrowed from the cool name Vince Marinaro gave his now-classic Letort river leaf-hopper fly imitations. That creation was a key fly for the launching of the American movement and love affair of fly fishing with terrestrials.

Leaf and tree hoppers are very small, compact, easily unnoticed terrestrials that are on many a trout's favorite spring, summer, and fall snack list. They actively jump amazing distances for their size and often hop and fly among ground and tree foliage that is adjacent to or over hanging trout waters. To my knowledge they, similar to ants, beetles, and many other terrestrials, do not come to water to drink but crash into the water accidentally or because of chilly temperatures or wind gusts. It can be difficult to identify when trout are taking leafhoppers. I've often gently stomach pumped trout that I thought were, because of their rise forms, midging or sipping small mayfly spinners . . . and surprisingly discovered they were loaded with tiny green or yellow leafhoppers!

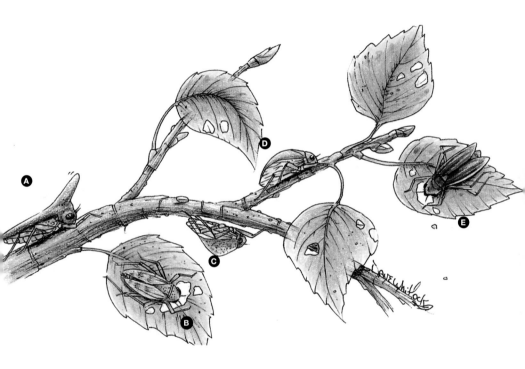

A. Some tree hoppers look like thorns.
B. Leaf and tree hoppers eat tree and plant leaves.
C. Most are colors that match their habitat.
D. The most common colors to match are yellow and light greens.
E. Some leaf hoppers are intricately and brightly colored.

In Arkansas, in the 1960s and early 1970s, the White and Norfork tailwater rivers were stacked up with big rainbows and browns. I watched many of these monsters make sporadic, slow rises on low-water, calm, sunny summer days, right in the middle of big pools. I tried all manner of surface dry flies without success, until I offered them a size 16, yellow-bodied, brown, palmer-hackled Marinaro's Jassid. About once every 20 or 30 long drifts over these huge fish, one would calmly elevator up 5 or 6 feet to just an inch under the Jassid, drift with it several feet, and then refuse it or slowly sip it down. The only problem was my seeing a dream fish under my fly and then controlling my adrenaline rush. I usually would not be able to wait and set too soon or too hard, or I'd give these 4- to 12-pound fish too much restraint and they'd pop my 6x tippet. I was finally able to land several each summer, with one just over 9 pounds, but I lost most. At that time I lacked the skill and lightweight

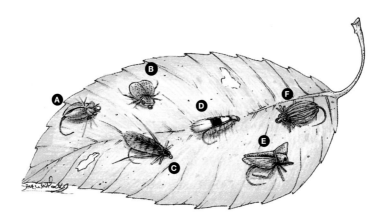

A. Foam and Swiss Straw leaf hopper

B. Sponge Rubber leaf hopper

C. Hackle (Hen) leaf hopper

D. Jassid

E. Balsa Wood tree hopper

F. Deer Hair leaf hopper

Leaf and tree hoppers provide trout with tasty little snacks from spring to late fall, but late summer and fall are when these insects are most abundant. Winds and chilly days drop most of them on the water.

tackle I needed to contend with such fish on 6x or 7x tippet. However, they are some of my most vivid trout memories. Today we are so fortunate to have the refinements in lines, leaders, rods, and reels to enjoy more consistent success fishing such tiny flies for big trout.

Leaf hoppers and tree hoppers usually have a predominately green or greenish-yellow color and some have very intricate and colorful markings on their backs. They have very compact bodies, short legs, hardly noticeable antenna, and no tails. I prefer to tie them in the fashion of Marinaro's original Jassid on short-shank, dry-fly hooks in sizes 12, 14, 16, and 18 (TMC 2487 BC). This hook gives me more bite for big

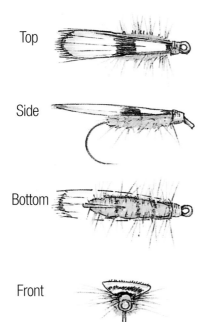

Top

Side

Bottom

Front

VINCE MARINARO'S CLASSIC JASSID

Note: Hackle is trimmed off of bottom to give fly a low surface film float and leaf hopper profile.

fish per fly size and makes the fly light on its belly and float low in the surface film.

The original Jassids were tied with the white-"eyed" jungle cock nail feather on the back, and this helps the fly fisher see it on the water. A small tuft of white or fluorescent yarn attached to the tippet near the fly also helps locate these diminutive, low-riding flies. Some fly fishers make leafhoppers out of buoyant foam, cork, or balsa wood. These materials are easier to obtain and less expensive than the jungle cock nail feathers.

You should fish leaf and tree hopper imitations with long, knotless, 5x to 8x Spring Creek type leaders. Try to avoid any drag, and when a trout rises to the fly, hold off—if you can—a second or two before making your smoothest, most delicate strike to get the highest percentage of hooking success. Also, don't apply much rod pressure initially to avoid a costly panic reaction by the fish, which can then cause a break-off.

I like a 1, 2, or 3 wt., 7'9"- to 8-foot, mid-action rod with a 12- to 15-foot, knotless, 5x to 8x leader. Think of yourself as a "trout whisperer" who is going to calmly coax a big trout to your hand or net.

Leaf and tree hoppers are available to trout from spring to late fall, but summer and early fall are probably the most productive times to imitate them. The finesse required for this delicate Jassid fishing, I believe, puts it on a par with—or perhaps even a more specialized level than—midging or fishing spinner tricos. And then there's the rewarding satisfaction that comes with catching a large selective trout that's softly feeding on tiny insects at the surface of slow-flowing, smooth water. I just get a really special tingle seeing a big nose poke through the surface film and sip down my little Jassid. See if you do too.

SIX

Fly Fishers' Matters

Dave Whitlock

THROUGH THE
TROUT'S EYES

Water—and the life forms living in it at its surface, in the water column, and along the bottom—has been an irresistible attraction for me since childhood. I've discovered over the years that virtually any puddle or pond, brook, stream, or river has a fascinating cycle revolving through it. For more than six decades, I've delved into the mystery and wonder of every stream that I've encountered. Now, I have an opportunity to share with readers what I've discovered about trout streams. My hope is not only to help you become a better angler but to also increase your knowledge of our living waters and perhaps show you even more ways to respect; treasure, conserve, and improve the trout's world, and in turn your own part of the world.

Air, land, and water are, of course, the three basic environments for living things on this earth. It's hard for land dwellers to have a true perspective of the life of those that spend most of their time in the other elements of air and water. My education and research have taught me a lot about trout, but it was only when I began to connect physically with wild trout in their environment that I began to truly understand how a trout sees, hears, smells, breathes, and moves in water, and how trout see our world.

My first lesson, when I was in my early twenties, was simply donning a swimsuit, with no face mask or fins, and submerging into a trout stream. Before I emerged their world, I had related to trout from a human perspective; that first contact was an astonishing experience, to say the least! I felt like I was in an alien world, and in a sense I was. Each new (and better equipped) entry into their watery habitat after that first one brought me closer to seeing the trout's world as a trout sees, experiences, and copes with it. It wasn't long before I was lying nearly motionless, submerged for hours to observe trout. I once spent almost three hours in Nelson's Spring Creek in Montana watching brown and rainbow trout feed on an emergence of pale morning duns. How amazing!

I began observing how fearful wild trout are of objects above them, especially moving objects, and sudden noises. The most startling to them seems to be the compounding movements and sounds an angler makes when wading toward a trout while casting over it, along with the noise of the fly line as it lands (or sometimes slaps) on the water. Some trout flee immediately; others sink to the bottom and hold there. In either case, the angler's goal—to interest the trout with a fly—is defeated. When I first started fly fishing in Montana's spring creeks and Yellowstone's Firehole River, I can remember many times seeing trout dash out of sight ahead of me. I caught very few of them back then.

Perhaps we just do not want to give trout credit for having the same instincts for survival as we grant wild turkey, deer, or fox. What we do *not* see, or perhaps don't take the time and patience to observe, is easy to misjudge. Spending a few hours watching a wild trout from above and below the water will teach you more about trout than several times that just fishing.

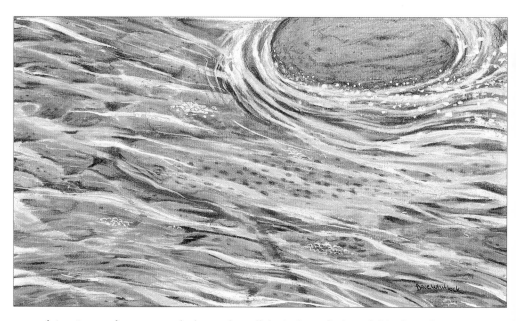

A trout seen from an angler's eye is a distorted, confusing sight of moving surface, floating objects, and dancing windows of light over mottled, camouflaged, vague, and compressed forms. Few, if any, of the trout's secrets are revealed.

Because we usually look only at the surface of a trout stream, our view of a trout's world is very distorted in terms of the fish's daily existence, its feeding positions, and the number of other trout in the vicinity and their moods and activities. The stream's surface, water color, and depth can restrict and distort our vision of trout so much that it takes extra effort, and polarized glasses, to get the real picture. A good habit is to stand quietly next to each stretch of water you plan to fish, and watch and listen for five to fifteen minutes. I know that sounds like a long time, but you'll be amazed at how much more you'll discover and how much more patiently and skillfully you will approach your quarry.

The same trout as seen through another trout's eyes (or a human's with a facemask underwater) clears and focuses the underwater scene and the forms within it. While the trout's underwater world is clear to itself, it views the surface through a distortion of bottom reflections and misleading surface views.

Water, being a trout's atmosphere, is infinitely more dense than our airy atmosphere, and the breathing movements, sight, hearing, smell, taste, and touch of trout have all evolved uniquely to make trout as efficient in water as we are on land or a bird is in flight. I now believe that to be a truly skilled trout angler and to appreciate and respect what a complicated treasure these fish are, you have to take the time to enter their world and observe them every chance you get.

RISE FORMS

ise forms are the particular configuration a trout makes as it rises and catches an insect in the water column, or near, at, or above the surface. Each group of aquatic insects has distinctive, often unique activities when transforming into adults or during mating and egg laying, which cause a trout to respond and catch the insects in a particular way. So each flash, swirl, break of the surface, or leap above it can be a key to the fly fisher that trout are actively feeding and which insect group and life-cycle stage they are taking.

Seven Rise Forms

The basic rise forms illustrated here are: the flash, swirl, hump, head-fin-tail, splash, leap, and sipping rise.

The *flash* is caused by a reaction to food that is near the bottom or just beginning to swim up the water column. With this rise form, trout are usually eating snails or cased caddis larvae on the bottom of

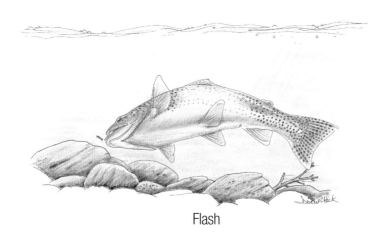

Flash

the stream, or nymphs that are just beginning to rise toward the surface. You'll usually see a quick, silver flash, but because of the water depth and distance from the fish, you'll seldom actually see the trout's form.

The *swirl* is similar to a flash, except the trout is rolling on its side, making a quick u-turn near the surface to seize an emerging nymph or pupa. The result is a flash, but it also includes a surface water disturbance from the trout's body and from the u-turn wash of its tail.

The *hump* or bulge is caused by the trout's "shoulders" (upper back) pushing smoothly through the surface and down again. It's an indication that the trout is feeding on or near the surface on drifting mayfly nymph emergers or midge pupa emergers.

The *head-fin-tail* rise indicates that a trout is feeding horizontally near the surface, sort of tipping up and dipping down as it takes emerging or surface-floating adult mayflies, stoneflies, and midges. This is the classically beautiful rise form we artists love to depict.

I remember one dark, snowy day in late October on a Montana spring pond thirty years ago. A couple dozen arm-long rainbows were

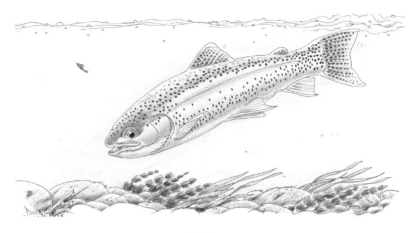

Swirl

Hump

daisy chaining around the pond like sharks, making slow head-fin-tail rises to a blanket hatch of black midges. I could see either their head, dorsal fin, or tail fin out of the water continuously. I managed to hook several of these monsters, but only landed one 31-incher on a 6x and a size 22 Adams. What a thrill!

Head-fin-tail

Dave's hint: You can usually tell a *head-fin-tail* rise from a hump rise by watching the area after the rise. If it's a head-fin-tail rise, you will usually see a bubble or two on the surface shortly after the trout gulps air while making an above-the-surface head-fin-tail rise. There is no bubble from the below-the-surface hump rise.

The *splash* rise is a sudden, noisy, water eruption caused by the headlong chase of a trout after the fast, missile-like launch of a caddis pupa into a flying adult. You'll usually see the trout's head and half or more of its body burst through the surface. Don't be tricked into tying on a floating elk-hair caddis. Often it's best to put on a wet fly, soft hackle, or caddis pupa, cast it near the splashy rise, let it sink, and then use the classic Leisenring lift.

The *leap* rise is when a trout leaps clear out of the water, usually when catching some sort of flying insect, especially damselflies, dragonflies, large stoneflies, mating caddis, or mayflies. This is a difficult rise form to fish to, but made much easier if you can recognize the target insect of

Splash

the leap and put that fly in the air near them. A good method to spot the flying insects is to get the sunlight between you and the insect—they'll be backlit and easier to see.

The *sipping* rise is sometimes called a "nose rise" or "smutting rise" and is one where the trout makes an almost imperceptible surface take. It's just a slow, gentle sip or suck action with its lips, usually just below the surface. Most often it occurs when trout are feeding on helpless, inactive,

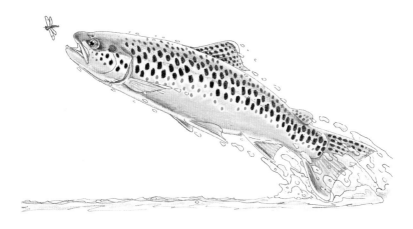

Leap

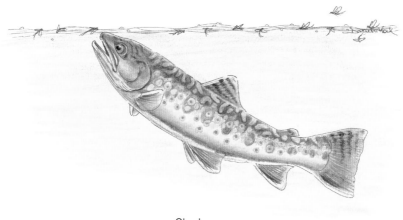

Sipping

spent adult mayflies, caddis, and midges. This rise is really deceptive because at the surface it looks like several small minnows or tiny trout feeding. After a hatch, a similar rise form takes place as trout pick off the last dead or crippled emergers stuck in the surface film.

Recognizing and understanding these seven rise forms will give you one more useful tool in your quest to match the hatch.

READING
TROUT WATER

My students often ask, "How do I know where trout are in a stream?" The term "reading the water" describes how an angler locates the best specific areas to catch fish. One must first recognize the seven basic gradients of a stream: waterfalls, rapids, riffles, runs, pools, flats, and the tails of the pools. Water, acted on by gravity, flows downhill at rates or speeds proportional to the extent of the gradients it flows over. The ability to recognize each gradient, which are common to all natural free-stone streams and most spring creeks and tailwarer rivers, will be a significant step in reading trout water.

Trout will locate in the gradients depending on what I call their "CSF" factor: comfort, safety and food. Gradients with optimum CSF factors will harbor more and larger trout. If a trout can't find a stream comfort zone that has the correct temperature (see the next chapter), ample oxygen and the right pH, it won't stay there. Within that zone, the fish must have reasonable safety from predators, as well as ample food.

When these three requirements coincide, you'll have an excellent fishing area.

I'll now describe each gradient in detail:

- *Waterfalls* are vertical drops from 12 inches up to many feet. They have no CSF value because of their speed, vertical position, and extreme turbulence. However, immediately downstream of most waterfalls lies a purge hole or pool that was dug by the fall's force. This area may have a fair CSF factor. Generally, fish concentrated here are temporary residents because the falls blocked their upstream movements. To catch trout from below waterfalls, cast upstream into the falls and let your fly sink and drift deep into the purge pool.

The Seven Gradients of a Trout Stream

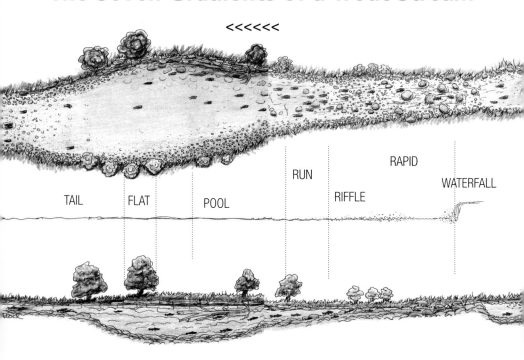

TAIL   FLAT   POOL   RUN   RIFFLE   RAPID   WATERFALL

- *Rapids* are high-gradient areas through which water flows swiftly and turbulently. They are noisy, filled with bubble and foam, and often too swift for trout and their food to reside comfortably. The CSF factors are very low. Smaller trout will hold in rapids if there are sufficient eddies behind and in front of larger rocks and boulders, but rapids are generally difficult places for most trout to find much CSF. Rapids tumbling down high-gradient mountain streams can be challenging for wading and fishing and require the utmost caution. The classic *"high stick, split-shot and nymph method"* or the *big, bushy dryflies around big boulders* are the best methods to entice trout to dash out from the slower water and snatch your fly.

- *Riffles* are moderately swift, shallow water that is choppy, noisy, and bubbly with a surface that appears to dance. They produce large amounts of oxygen and trout foods, so the CSF factor is high. Riffles are usually the easiest areas to locate and catch trout on flies, especially in the deeper sections and at the lower end where the water speed is slower. Because of the moderate speed, shallow depth, and abundance of oxygen created by the action, riffles are often where the largest amount of food forms live. The broken, choppy surface obscures visibility and helps protect trout from kingfishers, herons, and other predators.

Trout, invigorated by the high oxygen content and excited by a nearly constant movement of foods brought right to their holding positions, seem to feed here more consistently than in any other gradient. Riffles are classic fly-fishing areas from early spring to late fall for wading and fishing dry flies, wet flies, and nymphs. Small trout often reside in riffles, while larger trout position themselves in riffles mainly to feed.

- *Runs,* deeper, slower areas directly below riffles, have a lower gradient. The water is darker and the bottom is difficult to see from overhead. The surface of runs smooths out and the bubbles formed by the rapids or riffles clump together as foam lines floating with the current. The CSF factor is usually the highest in the run, especially at the upstream intersection with the riffle. Here trout, often the larger ones, concentrate to enjoy the abundant food from the riffles while having less energy-expending current with deeper, darker water for protection. Runs usually fish well year-round, especially with nymphs and streamers. With good hatches, they can offer excellent dry-fly fishing.
- *Pools* are deeper, wider, and much slower than the run, almost appearing to be stillwater. They are generally the result of the force of the swifter water from the waterfall, rapid, riffle, and run digging a deep depression. Trout are harder to locate in pools and somewhat harder to catch. Why? With deeper, slower water, the fish don't have to hurry to catch their food like they do in faster water; they get longer looks at drifting and swimming foods, and have a better chance to spot our deception.

Pools boast a moderately high CSF factor; after all, food is not as abundant or concentrated as in riffles and runs. Pools fish better if water is above normal level so that they have faster current and deeper water next to the shorelines. They are more productive very early or late in the day or at night. Pools are usually the best area to find fish concentrated when the water is very cold because chilled trout have a hard time moving fast and it takes less effort to swim in the slower water. Also, the water temperature is often a little warmer in deep water during cold weather. Fish pools with streamers and activated nymphs.

- *Flats* are flat, wide, shallow areas at the rear of pools. They have a low CSF factor and only fish well if there are enough concentrations of minnows, hatching insects, or windblown terrestrials to tempt out to venture from the pool to feed. Feeding is usually at night or during twilight. Flats require stealthy approaches to prevent trout from darting back into the pool.
- *Tails* are directly at the end of the pool where the shorelines constrict and the water smoothes and shallows, causing the current to speed up. It's a unique and difficult area to fish due to the difference in current speed, the smooth surface, and shallow water. The CSF factor is low and larger trout don't usually hold for long periods at the tail. The exception is when trout or steel head are migrating upstream and use the tail to rest or spawn. During these critical periods of a trout's life and reproductive cycle, avoid fishing the tails.

Trout Stream Temperature Management

T rout are classed as coldwater fish and flourish best in water that ranges between 45 and 65 degrees F. When water temperature rises to 70 and above, trout begin to lose their vitality and in time, will die. Global warming is and will continue to affect trout stream temperatures: as air temperatures increase, so do stream temperatures. There are numerous other situations that can also negatively affect trout water temperatures, such as too much exposure to the sun, low-flow levels, slow-flow rates, and the widening and/or shallowing of streams because of bank erosion caused by livestock, tree and shrub removal, in-stream gravel mining, etc. Until science, politicians, and we consumers come to a consensus and truly implement solutions that make a difference, you and I can help offset at least some of the warming of our

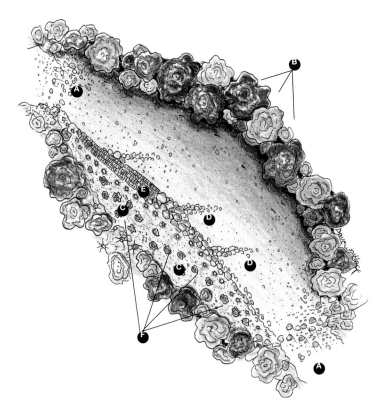

IMPROVING A SMALL STREAM TO KEEP IT COOLER, DEEPER, AND HABITAT RICH

A. Add coarse, large rocks to riffles to increase aeration and cooling needed in summer periods.

B. Mature, large deciduous and evergreen tree line.

C. Eliminate wide, shallow, slow flowing areas with D, E, and F.

D. Subsurface, rock-reef jetties direct the flow to center and encourage flow to dig the stretch deeper.

E. Large rock rip-rap or gabions.

F. Plant willows and fast-growing trees on the new shoreline to stabilize the bank and create more solar-shielding shade.

trout waters. We can do this by reducing some of these negative factors with hands-on, direct action to repair them and/or prevent as many of them as possible on the waters that are close to each of us.

Natural trout streams can become warmer if solar radiation is increased on a given volume of water. The more streams are shaded from spring, summer, and fall sunshine, the cooler they are. This is especially true for streams that are 100 feet wide or narrower.

Sunlit, shallow, slow-flowing water can warm 10 to 15 degrees F more than the same volume of water that is 70 to 80 percent shaded, deeper, and faster-flowing. So, if we can shade, narrow, deepen, and increase the flow rate, the water will be cooler and trout will be healthier, safer, and probably exist in larger numbers.

Shading Water

The following are four general types of shade that help the environment of a trout stream.

1. *Large adult trees*: Native deciduous trees such as oak, willow, sycamore, cottonwood and birch, are extremely beneficial in providing cooling shade during spring, summer, and early fall. They lose their leaves in late fall, allowing more sunlight on water in the winter when water temperatures need a bit of warming and aquatic plants need more light. Evergreens also provide excellent shade, but in most areas are best mixed with deciduous trees to allow the winter warming. Mature, streamside tree root systems are also very important for bank erosion control. *How you can help:* Protect new trees from

Young trees planted along stream banks:

(A) should have trunks armored against chewing with 1 x 2-inch hardware cloth wire.

(B) need watering the first year. Try to form a mulch basin around each to catch and hold water better.

indiscriminant cutting and from extensive chewing damage by wildlife. One alternative is to protect each tree with a 1-inch by 2-inch hardware cloth (heavy-gauge wire) cage around the base. In summer, note where the stream receives long periods of direct sunlight and then in early fall, plant native trees in these areas. They will grow quickly and provide shade over the stream. Remember to protect their tender trunks and water them often the first year. In many areas, if they are native, willows can be propagated by cutting pieces of willow branches or trunks that are 2 inches or more in diameter and 3 feet or more in length and then pushing them into the ground along the bank.

2. *Shrubs*: When located on the edge of a stream, native shrubs that grow up to 20 feet, such as dogwood, redbud, rhododendron, alder, mountain laurel, and cedar, provide dense shade, habitat for food sources, and overhead protection to trout. The roots also hold bank soils in place. *How you can help:* Choose species native to your area and plant them, with wire protectors, along barren banks if beavers are present, in fall or early spring. Provide regular water in the first year.

3. *Grasses and flowering plants*: Heavy plant cover on trout stream banks is essential to prevent erosion during floods and to provide habitat for terrestrial insects and safe harbor for resting, adult aquatic insects. These smaller plants establish faster than trees and shrubs, so are an ideal quick fix where trout stream banks are barren of plant growth due to flooding, fire, erosion, or overgrazing livestock. *How you can help:* You can obtain native grass seed and wildflower mixes from local farm stores, your county agriculture agent, or fish and game departments. Be sure to use native seeds, ideally from the local area. Some non-native species can be very invasive and can eventually crowd out important native species. Depending on your location and type of seeds, plant in fall or spring for best results. **Whenever possible, restrict livestock from random access to stream banks.**

These animals destroy valuable streamside growth and create excessive bank erosion.

4. *Water structures*: Large underwater rocks, logs, and smaller rocks have an infinite value in trout streams for providing subsurface shade, bottom stabilization, fish and insect protection, and oxygen enhancement. *How you can help:* Properly chosen, native aquatic plants can add significantly to water shading, fish cover, oxygen

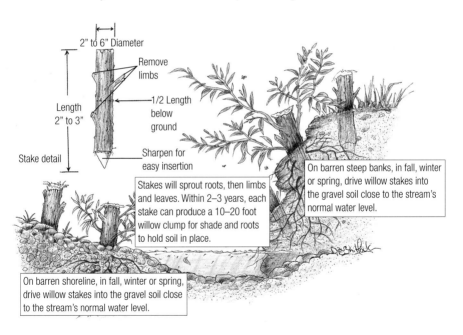

Cut sections 2–3 feet long from live willow trees. Remove limbs and bury or drive into stream banks up to 1/2 length of stake.

2" to 6" Diameter

Remove limbs

Length 2" to 3"

1/2 Length below ground

Stake detail

Sharpen for easy insertion

Stakes will sprout roots, then limbs and leaves. Within 2–3 years, each stake can produce a 10–20 foot willow clump for shade and roots to hold soil in place.

On barren steep banks, in fall, winter or spring, drive willow stakes into the gravel soil close to the stream's normal water level.

On barren shoreline, in fall, winter or spring, drive willow stakes into the gravel soil close to the stream's normal water level.

content, and trout food habitat. Check your stream's plant types and growth, and if the vegetation is lacking, consult your local state fishing biologist for the information and permission to obtain the *right* aquatic plants for your waters. You may lose a few flies to this valuable vegetation, but in terms of more and healthier trout, the payoff is worth it.

Large rocks in riffles, runs, and heads of pools, where trout can hold beside or beneath, provide excellent shade, breaks from holding in current, and "streamscaping" for trout. When occurring in groups or series, rocks can enhance the stream flow rate and stabilize both sides of the stream. You'll need a nearby local source, three or four stout backs or a small backhoe to place the rocks. Wooden pallets, cinder blocks, or smaller rocks, placed under and hidden by the larger rocks, provide good support for big rocks and allow the 6 to 12 inches of space beneath for trout to hide under.

Properly placed wood structures, such as tree trunks, stumps, and root wads, can provide trout with direct shade, current breaks, deeper water, and overhead and horizontal predator protection, as well as bank stabilization. Most trout streams have good sources of these woody structures close by. They must be properly placed and anchored, or they can cause flow and silt problems or be lost in high water. In general, woody structures work best on the deep side of runs and pools that lack large rock or overhead tree structures.

Additional Temperature Controls

Make riffles more turbulent with groups of medium to large rocks partially exposed above the surface. This creates more cooling evaporation and a lot more vital aeration, especially in warmer months for trout. Cooler turbulent water absorbs and transfers more *oxygen* than warmer, non-bubbling water flowing at the same rate of speed. These larger rocks can also help stabilize riffle erosion and provide better habitat for aquatic insects, minnows, and small trout.

Another way to gain cooler water is to make parts of a stream narrower and deeper and increase the water exchange in pools. Some shallows are necessary, but those wide, shallow, slow-flow sections of a stream can heat up quickly in warm weather and/or sunlight. You can drop the temperature of a stream as much as 5 degrees F by eliminating some of these problem areas.

Extending and building up the shallow bank side with coarse rock, gabions, riprap, and fast-growing trees like willows can narrow a stream. When the stream becomes narrower, the flow increases and the water deepens. This faster flowing, deeper water holds a cooler temperature better.

You, your fishing friends, or your Trout Unlimited chapter can make a significant improvement to your local trout stream temperature management and environment if you'll implement some of these suggestions. Be forewarned: some of the activities discussed here, such as placing large boulders in streams, may require permits from state or federal agencies, so check with local water quality and land use agencies for necessary permission. Private stream environmental consultants and services are also available and easy to find on the Internet.

Remember, even a little improvement makes a difference.

HOW TO ELIMINATE SHALLOW AREAS TO DEEPEN, COOL, AND STABILIZE A STREAM

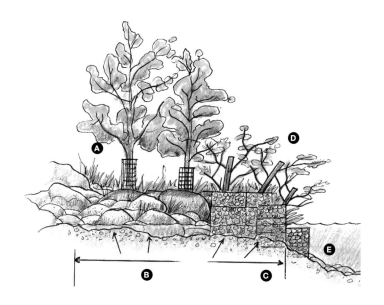

A. Young trees, armored with wire
B. Large rocks and boulders
C. Gabions
D. Willow plugs
E. Underwater gabions

TROUT STREAM TEMPERATURE MANAGEMENT

STEPS TO TEMPERATURE CONTROL

A. Mature deciduous and evergreen trees for major solar radiation shielding of stream water

B. Shrubs provide close, dense shade and overhead protection for trout, as well as habitat for insects that trout feed on.

C. Grasses, ferns and vines, another source of shade, bank cover and fish-food habitat.

D. Logs lashed and anchored into bank—source of dense, direct shade and excellent overhead protection for trout

E. Large rocks and boulders with space underneath for shade and protection

F. Aquatic vegetation for shade and protection plus production of oxygen, CO_2 absorption and trout food production

G. Tree, shrub, and grass root systems hold shoreline in place to keep banks stable

Stream that is narrower, deeper, and exchanges water volumes stays much cooler.

Water Temperatures and Seasonal Locations of Fish

Key to successful fishing, water temperature is also one of the most important of all the factors involved in a trout's health. Why? First, trout are cold-*water* species and for optimum survival, require water temperature between 45 and 65 degrees F. Second, trout are cold-*blooded*, which means that they, unlike us warm-blooded humans, cannot maintain constant body temperatures. For trout, water temperature controls body temperature. Generally speaking, as water temperatures rise through the 45- to 65-degree range, a trout's metabolism increases, spurring an increase in growth rate, and mental, muscular, and digestive functions.

This steady increase in metabolism maxes out for trout at 58 to 65 degrees F, after which the higher temperatures begin to depress a trout's metabolism. This is mainly because of the way that oxygen is released from water as temperatures rise. The warmer the water, the less oxygen content; likewise, the colder the water, the more oxygen it can hold. So at temperatures above 70 to 75 degrees F, the water generally will not contain enough oxygen for trout to function correctly.

Oxygen does not naturally occur much in water. It must be injected or dissolved by either agitation where the water and air meet, such as a rocky riffle or raindrops hitting the water surface, or by photosynthesis caused by the sun hitting aquatic vegetation. Air normally contains about 21 percent oxygen. Under ideal temperatures and barometric conditions (i.e., high barometric pressure and temperatures in the low 30s), oxygen in water will reach its maximum concentration of around 15 parts per million (ppm). As the water temperature rises, molecular activity increases and the oxygen molecules escape faster from the water into the air. The ppm of dissolved oxygen in water versus water temperature is complex, but for our purposes, 8 to 9 ppm in 45- to 65-degree water is considered ideal. Trout cannot survive well in water with 3 ppm or less dissolved oxygen, which usually occurs when water temperatures reach the higher 70s. For humans, imagine trying to breathe and work above 15,000 or 20,000 feet in elevation. At those altitudes, oxygen deficiency curtails almost all physical functions.

When water is below 45 degrees F, and especially in the 30s, a trout's metabolism really slows down. Trout swim more slowly, have less strength and endurance, and their senses are depressed. Can you recall a time when your hands got so cold you began to lose dexterity and couldn't tie a fly on your line? A cold trout experiences much the same condition when chilled below 40 degrees, except over its entire body! The fish have plenty of oxygen, but because they are the same temperature as the water, they are simply too cold to function well. They even have trouble catching and grasping food morsels, especially in swift water or if the food is quickly animated or moving irregularly. Trout confined to waters that are cold (30 to 50 degrees) usually grow more slowly, tend to take more time to mature and seldom become large; however, they seem to live longer.

When fishing while water temperatures are in the low 40s and 30s, use small flies and move them slowly, consistently, and as close to a trout's nose as possible. Delay setting the hook so that a lethargic trout has time to take the fly into its mouth.

As water temperatures begin to rise above the optimum and water oxygen content decreases, trout almost cease to metabolize, eat less, and lose weight. In sustained, warm water conditions (70 to 75 degrees), this lack of oxygen causes their body functions, such as digestion, muscle strength, and immunity to fungus, bacteria and disease, to drop severely; eventually death occurs. When temperatures reach 80 to 85 degrees, trout suffocate from lack of oxygen. I've witnessed trout thriving in warm water, but they are in areas that get a super charge of agitation with air, like

WATER TEMPERATURES AND SEASONAL LOCATIONS OF TROUT

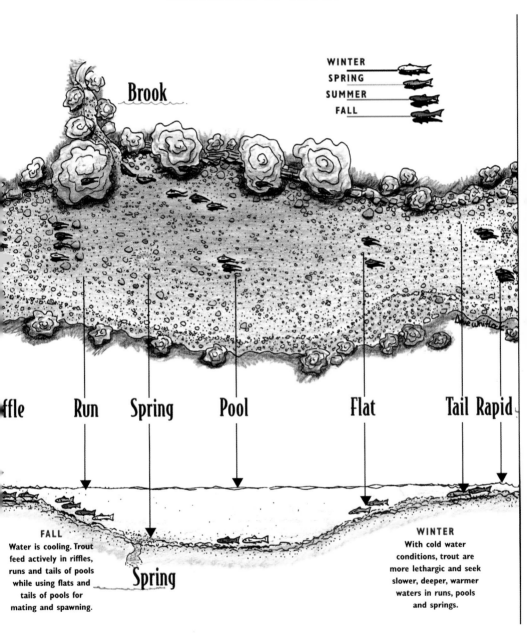

Brook

WINTER
SPRING
SUMMER
FALL

ffle   Run   Spring   Pool   Flat   Tail Rapid

Spring

FALL
Water is cooling. Trout feed actively in riffles, runs and tails of pools while using flats and tails of pools for mating and spawning.

WINTER
With cold water conditions, trout are more lethargic and seek slower, deeper, warmer waters in runs, pools and springs.

a waterfall or strong rapids. Unique unto themselves are the Fire Hole River trout in Yellowstone National Park. These fish seem to have evolved in this geothermally heated river and have a high tolerance for the low oxygen levels associated with the Fire Hole's high water temperatures (75 to 90 degrees).

When fishing while water temperatures exceed 65 degrees, trout are increasingly stressed when hooked and played, then handled and released. Excess lactic acid buildup and oxygen depletion can be lethal to a released trout, even if it displays the strength to swim away upright. I'd advise refraining from fishing for trout in warm water conditions; at the very least, be sure to land them quickly and never remove their heads from the water. When the gills of a trout are lifted out of the water, the fish cannot take in oxygen.

Trout, especially wild trout, will seek out the most ideal water temperatures, even if they have to move considerable distances. Even freshly stocked, domesticated hatchery trout will search locally for the best comfort zones. Usually this search first occurs in late winter and early spring to find warmer water or water that makes fewer physical demands. Deep, slow pools don't require much swimming effort, while springs; groundwater seepage; shallow, sunny areas; and the bases of tailwater dams offer warmer waters and some relief from winter's cold effects.

Late spring, summer, and early fall often provide too much solar heating. Trout then seek out springs and groundwater seepage; cooler brook inlets; shady areas; deeper, cooler pools; middle-flows of riffle runs; rapids or waterfalls; and tailwaters. Springs, groundwater seepages, and areas below tailwater dams attract trout in both cold- and warm-water seasons because they usually flow somewhere between 42 and 56 degrees all year long. But because springs are often void of oxygen and/or have too much nitrogen, trout may locate a short distance from their entrances where oxygen and nitrogen levels are better because of blending with the stream water.

I always carry a waterproof digital thermometer to check water temperatures where I trout fish. This simple, inexpensive instrument will quickly give you the most relevant data on *where* trout will be and how *active* they will be toward your lures and flies.

I hope the thoughts and information in this book help you to better understand and enjoy the fascinating world of trout.

ACKNOWLEDGMENTS

This book was made possible because of Nick Lyons, my wife Emily, and Trout Unlimited. Nick, a longtime friend and the editor of my other books, encouraged Trout Unlimited to invite me to write and illustrate the Artful Angler series for *Trout Magazine*. TU has allowed me, with very few restrictions, to explore the world of trout with my pen and paints, and they gave their permission to reprint the series in this book. Emily's enthusiasm and support of my work and her superb editing of each chapter are perhaps the most significant factors leading to this book's existence. Thank you all so much.

—Dave

INDEX